Direct Work with Vulnerable Children

of related interest

Communication Skills for Working with Children and Young People
Introducing Social Pedagogy
3rd edition
Pat Petrie
ISBN 978 1 84905 137 8
eISBN 978 0 85700 331 7

Working with Children and Teenagers Using Solution Focused Approaches
Enabling Children to Overcome Challenges and Achieve their Potential
Judith Milner and Jackie Bateman
ISBN 978 1 84905 082 1
eISBN 978 0 85700 261 7

Empathic Care for Children with Disorganized Attachments
A Model for Mentalizing, Attachment and Trauma-Informed Care
Chris Taylor
ISBN 978 1 84905 182 8
eISBN 978 0 85700 398 0

Life Story Therapy with Traumatized Children
A Model for Practice
Richard Rose
Foreword by Bruce D. Perry, M.D., Ph.D.
ISBN 978 1 84905 272 6
eISBN 978 0 85700 574 8

Therapeutic Residential Care for Children and Young People
An Attachment and Trauma-Informed Model for Practice
Susan Barton, Rudy Gonzalez and Patrick Tomlinson
Foreword by Brian Burdekin
ISBN 978 1 84905 255 9
eISBN 978 0 85700 538 0

Recognizing and Helping the Neglected Child
Evidence-Based Practice for Assessment and Intervention
Brigid Daniel, Julie Taylor and Jane Scott
With David Derbyshire and Deanna Neilson
Foreword by Enid Hendry
ISBN 978 1 84905 093 7
eISBN 978 0 85700 274 7
Safeguarding Children Across Services series

Social Work with Children and Families
Getting into Practice
3rd edition
Ian Butler and Caroline Hickman
ISBN 978 1 84310 598 5
eISBN 978 0 85700 556 4

Learning Through Child Observation
2nd edition
Mary Fawcett
ISBN 978 1 84310 676 0
eISBN 978 1 84642 964 4

Direct Work with Vulnerable Children

Playful Activities and Strategies for Communication

Audrey Tait and Helen Wosu

Jessica Kingsley *Publishers*
London and Philadelphia

First published in 2013
by Jessica Kingsley Publishers
116 Pentonville Road
London N1 9JB, UK
and
400 Market Street, Suite 400
Philadelphia, PA 19106, USA

www.jkp.com

Library of Congress Cataloging in Publication Data
Tait, Audrey, 1970-
  Direct work with vulnerable children : playful activities and strategies for
communication / Audrey Tait
and Helen Wosu ; foreword by Brigid Daniel.
     p. cm.
  Includes bibliographical references and index.
  ISBN 978-1-84905-319-8 (alk. paper)
  1. Social work with children. 2. Children--Services for. 3. Play therapy. I. Wosu,
Helen, 1945- II. Title.
  HV713.T28 2013
  362.71'6--dc23
                          2012027543

British Library Cataloguing in Publication Data
A CIP catalogue record for this book is available from the British Library

ISBN 978 1 84905 319 8
eISBN 978 0 85700 661 5

Printed and bound in Great Britain

To all the children and young people we have worked with, some of the bravest and most inspirational people we have met.

Acknowledgements

This book is the creative work of Audrey Tait, who has been developing activities for some of the most vulnerable children in society in order to give them a voice.

It has been knocked into shape by Helen Wosu, who first met Audrey working in a social work practice team six years ago and was bowled over by her compassion and creativity. Audrey shows us that we can learn the skills to build relationships with the neediest children to positively affect outcomes for them, perhaps best put by a parent, who, when asked by Audrey for permission to use a case study said 'I'll do anything for you Audrey as you've turned our lives around.'

Both Audrey and Helen are grateful to their parents for providing the kind of childhoods that have helped them weather life's storms, giving encouragement and acceptance in abundance.

The authors wish to say a big thank you to Celia Eighteen who has patiently chased and corrected errant verbs and apostrophes throughout the book. Any errors that remain are their responsibility.

Lastly both authors would like to thank colleagues and managers at the City of Edinburgh Council who have supported their work and made this book possible.

Note: To protect anonymity all names and identifying features have been changed in theis book. Also, to avoid gender stereotyping, and in keeping with publishers' practice, we use alternate genders by chapter throughout the book.

Contents

Chapter 1
Engaging Effectively with Children

Sometimes children suffer longer than they should in environments that are stressful, abusive and unsafe because the adults around them lack the skills to open the door to effective communication.

For the past four years I have been sharing my tool bag of games and activities, developed over 20 years in practice, in a training course for social workers in Edinburgh, called Communicating with Children. Colleagues realised that these tools were effective and filled a critical learning gap in social work education. This book was born out of requests for written material from social workers, police officers, foster carers, nursery nurses, residential care officers and others attending the course. Engaging effectively with children requires skill and commitment, but it is a skill that can be learned, and these activities will help build your confidence and give you practical ideas and resources to use.

Social workers frequently have to work with children to address very difficult issues. It is often the first time they have met the child. It is important to keep in mind that the world view of children who have been abused and neglected is likely to be that the adults around them neither care about them nor have been able to protect them, and may have been the abusers themselves (Ainsworth *et al.* 1978). In these circumstances, it is imperative that we are able to convey to the child that we are safe, caring and interested adults.

When engaged in long-term work, there are additional challenges in building and sustaining a relationship with a child. Children who have been consistently let down by adults often build a protective barrier that means they are very cautious of, or even closed down to, investing in a relationship. It is not uncommon for a child to try very hard not to engage with a worker, to reject the possibility of a relationship almost before it has begun. For these children, experience of multiple losses has shown that it can be unsafe to trust (Fahlberg 1991). Their experience is that they have to attempt to self-regulate, to be emotionally self-sufficient, which, for an immature brain, often results in defensiveness on the one hand, or being emotionally over-demanding (Gerhardt 2004) on the other.

With every interaction we have with a child we have the power to begin to change this world view of adults, whether we are foster carers, social workers, teachers, nursery nurses or care workers. In effect, we can offer children a different working model of the world. This healing process can begin with the child learning to engage and trust just one other person in her life. You could be that person. This is a huge privilege and also a huge responsibility, but in my experience the rewards and benefits are immeasurable, for both the child and the worker.

This was perhaps best conveyed to me recently by a young man in his twenties. I had worked with him when he was 14–16 years old and quite early on he told me that his philosophy of life was D.T.N. – Don't Trust No one. This was the safest way to be, he told me, so you wouldn't get hurt. He had a poor view of social workers, but I was committed to offering consistent and caring support, and gradually a working relationship developed between us. On ending my work with him, I encouraged him to let me know how he was getting on and indeed, after about six months, he contacted me to tell me his news. A few years passed and the next time I met him was when I was helping in a soup kitchen for the homeless. He recognised me immediately and thanked me for the work I had done with him as a teenager. He reflected that he had not liked or trusted me initially but had grown to feel he could depend on me, and said there had been no one else in his life he had felt that way about. He ended by stating, 'You did a lot for me 'cos I knew you were there. Even if you couldn't fix stuff you were there with me.'

With a little encouragement he shared with me his current problems and we were able to work out some strategies to solve some of the practical ones. At the end of that conversation he said, 'I am no a kid now, Audrey, but I feel like I did when you worked with me. Like I'm not alone.'

He still keeps in touch every so often, telling me his current news. His calls are often not more than five minutes but I believe that is enough for him to feel connected to someone.

This book is primarily a set of playful activities to create opportunities to engage children (and sometimes adults). Through these activities, children are enabled to tell you their stories and provide you with assessment opportunities, but ultimately the best way to help, support and heal children is through offering them a caring, nurturing and safe relationship. Don't be put off if your early attempts are rejected – just keep offering. Never give up, for the benefits to both the receiver and giver are so great. They are life changing – you can change children's lives and they will certainly change yours.

Most of these activities presented in this book will take 30–45 minutes (roughly the time allotted to a home visit), although it will largely depend on the child's presentation, stage of development and level of interest. Some of the activities could be extended over two or three sessions.

Chapter 2

Preparation

Confidentiality

Children have the right to confidentiality during one-to-one sessions. However, it would be naive to think this can be absolute. Issues will arise in the course of working with a child that do need to be shared with others – either with the child's immediate carers or, in the case of child protection, other professionals and potentially the child's own family members.

The important thing is to be honest with the child from the start. The child's developmental age will determine how you explain the level of confidentiality that you can offer (and this may also depend on your role). With younger children, I talk about safe and fun secrets, 'like when you have made a card for mummy and you don't want to tell her before her birthday'. I tell the child that we all like those kinds of secrets. But there are other secrets that are upsetting, maybe about the child or someone else getting hurt or not being safe. These kinds of things can't be kept secret because they are too big for anybody to have to keep secret. We have to tell these secrets, so we call them 'have to tell secrets'.

I usually have this conversation using a series of picture cards and discussing which ones could be secrets. Why would they be secret? Are they 'fun secrets' or 'have to tell secrets'?

For children who can read well, having short scenarios written down can be more developmentally appropriate. In group work you could ask one group to act out the secret and one to discuss whether they think it is a 'fun secret' or a 'have to tell secret'. Do both groups agree?

Issues will arise in sessions that you either need to tell main carers or that would be beneficial to tell. In this situation I acknowledge this with the child and explain why I think it would be a good idea to tell.

In a situation where it would be beneficial to tell, I invite the child to tell the carer/parent with me and let the child do the talking while I am present, as support. If this is not comfortable for the child, I will speak to the carer/parent myself, preferably in the child's presence. If the child doesn't want to be there, or leaves half way through, that is fine. I just recap what I told the carer with the child before I leave, or later, in a letter. I usually write this in the form of a cartoon or picture written in colourful felt tip pen. Older children may prefer a formal, more adult letter, or even a text.

If the child chooses not to tell the carer, I will hold off telling until the next session and ask the child again if we could tell the carer/parent and explain the benefits, as I see them, of doing this.

When it is a situation where we *need* to tell the carer (for example, something that has an impact on the child's safety) I would say to the child that we need to tell and explain clearly why. I would also be clear that even if the child didn't consent, I would tell the carer (and anyone else who had to be informed). Again, the aim should be to involve the child as far as possible.

Think about your appearance

Try to wear something that might attract a child's interest or imagination and gives the message that you are child friendly. For example, I have made a colourful, beaded watchstrap that I wear. Young children enjoy looking at the beads, holding it and trying it on. Older girls also consider it to be cool, as beads are in fashion. I may also wear an interesting badge or brooch. Men could wear a colourful tie or maybe carry a novelty key ring (but better not one with car/house keys on it as they could go astray).

All children subconsciously scan adults. They look for clues. This is normal developmental behaviour, particularly in the early years. The trick is to be aware of this and help the process by giving clues that tell the child, 'I like similar things to you!'

The best teachers and nursery staff understand this. I had the privilege of meeting a teacher who had attached fabric cherries to her shoes because one of her most challenging children (who happened to be my client) had loved a story about a cherry tree. In a bid to engage this girl, she had decorated her shoes, and the first thing the child told me when I met her in school was, 'Ma teacher's got cherry shoes, Audrey!'

Use of language

The language we use is very important in all settings and in a number of ways.

To begin, let's consider how I use language. I use the word 'children', yet I always emphasise when training that most of the tools and my playful approach can be used with 'young people' (and often adults). I deliberately apply the term children in reference to anybody under the age of 16. There is a reason for this.

In the past few years I have been struck by the expectations we place on young people and by the very unforgiving attitude many adults appear to adopt towards them. Regardless of developmental age (often much below chronological age in neglected and abused children) or their traumatic life experiences, these young people, when they reach 12 or 13, are expected to behave like young adults. No wonder they fail.

So when using the term 'young people', don't forget that it is developmentally normal for them to be like children in many ways, as vulnerable children often have a younger developmental age than their peers. It is right that our young people are given more responsibility. It is right to encourage and support them to make choices and decisions more independently and to give them the experience of consequence and action, but they still need adults' care and protection, love and encouragement, and we need to remember that they are essentially still children, albeit older children. So my first principle when speaking to other professionals about a 'young person' is to use the word 'child' at some point early on. The term tends to elicit a more caring and protective response as well as hope and optimism, which all children need.

Language delay

It is no coincidence that many of the children we work with have delayed language. Advances in neuroscience inform us that there is a window of opportunity for language development in our early years. Our ability with words is dependent on the care and opportunities we are given. Children learn about language from the moment they are born, including learning to recognise different caregivers' voice tones. If the carers have difficulties in their lives that prevent them from communicating effectively with their baby, the child is disadvantaged from birth in the opportunity to learn and utilise language. Equally, children who have not had the experience of being listened to nor indeed the opportunity to have positive, constructive conversations can sometimes shut down to language. They haven't found it to be useful, so no longer fully engage with it. This is problematic when the principal way of communicating with children is through speech and language. So it is not surprising that children often don't respond well to formal (forensic) interviews where the medium of communication is only through speech and language, and that language more suited to adults than to children. However, if you support appropriate language for a child's development and culture with play, including visual tools, you can open the gateway to good communication.

Culture

Language is influenced by the child's development and culture. It may seem obvious but I make no apology for including it because it is so often forgotten. A foster carer told me about an emergency placement of a three-year-old. The foster carer said the placing social worker was very kind and had even made an effort to buy clothes, but she didn't know basic information about the child, such as the word the child used for going to the toilet. 'The wee one kept asking me for a "keek"', the foster carer told me, 'so I kept playing peek-a-boo with him and he eventually soiled his pants and said in distress, "See, told you me need a keek"'.

It is these small details that could have prevented the humiliation this particular boy felt. Not only that, but it also sent a message in the initial hours of placement that his carer did not understand him and was unable to meet some of his needs.

I always check out with all the children I work with the words they use in their daily lives. Do they have a 'nana' or a 'granny'? Do they have 'friends' or 'homies'? Do they go home for their 'tea' or their 'dinner'? Do they feel 'fed up' or is their 'heid chapping' (do they feel stressed)? It's good to check these things out as early as possible in your relationship and at a time when the child is relaxed and you can laugh together about the differences and turn it into a game. Older children are usually happy to educate you in their language. Then, when you are working with them, you will find that if you use the same words it will ease the communication between you. With very young children, you should get this information from the child's main carers.

It is also important to note that children's language development is influenced by their life experiences and knowledge base. I worked with a nine-year-old and we were talking about the important people in her life (using the *Candle Work* activity, see pp.187–90). She named one of them as her 'granddad' but said, 'He's dead though.' I said we could still make a candle for him, and she continued:

Child: 'What happened to his body?'

Me: 'Well I am not sure. Sometimes people's bodies are buried and they help the grass and trees to grow. Sometimes there is a cremation. That means that the person's body is made into ashes and put in a very special jar so that their family can keep them in a safe place. I am not sure what happened to your granddad's body. We could ask mum if you would like to know.'

Child: 'Which way is best?'

Me: 'Well, both are good. We have to do something with a body that doesn't work anymore.'

Child: 'Mum said his soul went to heaven.'

Me: 'Yes, I believe people's souls go to heaven too.'

Child: 'But why the souls?'

Me: 'Because that is the most important part of the person. It is the part that loves – the part that makes you who you are.'

Child (looking at feet): 'Really?'

Me (the penny drops): 'Ah, did you think mum meant the soles of your feet?'

Child nods and I explain.

There is a rich diversity of language and expression within many of the societies we work in and also between families sharing the same culture. Always be alert to this and ask if you don't understand. Equally, encourage people to ask if they don't understand you. Professionals are guilty of using jargon and not even realising it.

Listening

Children have lots of valuable and important things to tell us. They are the experts on their life story and they often have or can find creative solutions to the dangers they face in their lives. All we need to do is support them to tell us and *listen*. Listening is not just about the spoken word but also takes into account messages children convey to us through play, drawings or behaviour. I may not be clear about what that message is, but I can reflect back to the child what he is doing or showing me, in the same way you would reflect back statements in person-centred counselling (Rogers 2003).

For example, if a child was playing with two toy figures, making one jump upon the other, I would say, 'Wow you're making one man jump hard on the other man and the other man is lying still. You're making some loud noises too.' In that way I convey to the child that I am with him in his play and that I am attentive and listening. I am also checking out my understanding. It is important not to read into children's play, however. It is often symbolic and provides the child with the opportunity to work through things he has seen or experienced, or sometimes it can simply be he is just expressing his imagination. Few of us who work with children are therapists, and also we may not know the context of the play, so while it is wise to observe closely, note the child's actions and check out any concerning issues that arise, it is unwise to assume you understand completely what is being demonstrated. In my experience, when children play out an incident they have witnessed or experienced, there will be a lot of fine detail and often an understanding beyond their years. Their language in play may sound more adult and you may hear them repeat precise phrases or mimic tones of voice. Some children will also have a strong emotional response or physical reaction and may become very animated and rushed in play. They may repeat the same sequence a number of times. They may also require nurturing responses from you like a drink, seeking comfort or needing to go to the toilet.

The result is often that the child then tells you more about his play or includes you in his play. When at all possible, act on what the children tell you. Show them that you value them; demonstrate to them that you care about them. For example, when one of the children told me through play with small dolls that she felt left out at playtime because she didn't have a snack, I gave the child an apple that I had with me. I spoke to the parent about providing a snack and checked with the school a day later to see if this had happened. It hadn't, so I telephoned the parent and we agreed that for the remainder of that week I would place a bag of snacks in the school and the classroom assistant would give one to the child each day. The agreement was that the following week the parent would take up this responsibility. I have heard it argued that this is taking over parental responsibility, creating dependency for the parent. However, the child was my client and not having a snack was causing her distress in her world. It was a very important issue and was linked to how she socialised with her peers. In practising in a child-centred way, I prioritised the child's need at that particular time. It was less important who provided the snack.

This issue was important for the child in the short term but it also gave me an opportunity to demonstrate to the child that I would act on concerns she had and therefore I hoped she would have confidence in me in the future if she had other worries or problems. It is also worth remembering that adults who have a history of alcohol or substance misuse may well have damaged areas of the brain which affects their memory and ability to plan, and so require reminders and assistance to develop these skills (for example, keeping a diary/journal) to help build new brain connections.

The little girl's willingness to go to school improved during the week when I provided the snacks. The following week the headteacher called me to tell me that once again the child had come to school with no snack. The next morning I did an unannounced visit to the family before the school day began and gave the mother and the little girl a lift to the Co-op store to buy five snacks (the mother paid for them), and we left them in the school office. This took only half an hour out of my working day. The next week, the mother brought five snacks into school on the Monday morning. Recognising that the mother's emotional development was younger than her chronological years, I heaped praise on her for managing this, and by the third week she was providing them on a daily basis, going to the shop each day before school. This was initiated by the little girl, who suggested to her mother that doing it that way would be easier, and that they would meet other mothers doing the same thing.

The underlying principle is that I listened to the child's agenda. For her, having no snack was a big issue, affecting attendance and social ease with her peers. My actions gave her the message not only that I listened and placed importance on the things that she identified as important in her life, but also that I tried to fix it and that I was reliable in following through on promises. It also demonstrated to her that while I was respectful of her mother, I knew that her mother did not always do the things the little girl needed her to do. All of the above were powerful and important messages. This child was suffering from neglect and emotional abuse. In further sessions she was able to talk to me about her mother's drug addiction and behaviour while under the influence of drugs, despite being warned by her mother not to tell. I believe this was only possible because we had found an effective way to communicate that felt safe and because I had demonstrated to her that I valued her and could effect change.

Chapter 3

Free Play

The aim here is to convince you that free play is not an activity confined to therapists or children's nursery workers. It is a powerful and invaluable tool for building relationships that allows you to support children effectively. For years I have been working this way in a busy statutory social work practice team where time is scarce and pressures are heavy.

One of the best ways to develop a helping relationship with children is to support their free play. This, for some adults, is not as easy as it sounds, but like all skills, it can be learned, and in my opinion, is essential for children's workers.

When children feel safe and they trust you, given the right opportunities they will communicate to you what is happening in their world. Please note, I didn't say *tell* you. Children will sometimes simply have a conversation, but often they will initially show you through play. Also note I said, 'what is happening in their world'. A young child may not have much exposure to the wider world, so she is likely to believe that everybody's experience mirrors her own. While we know that not everybody's mother injects heroin, children may not know this. They may feel scared by their mothers' behaviour but assume all mothers behave like that. From a child's perspective adults know everything and don't need to be told.

It is through play that children make sense of their experiences and try to learn and understand the world, so it is highly likely they will play out experiences that are causing them unease (as well as all the good healthy experiences they have). It is our job to meet children where they are, and to facilitate communication. Only then can we protect and advocate.

Our role as adults is to provide a rich variety of play materials. A playroom is the ideal location for this. Allow the child to dictate what to play with and how to play with that material. Remain beside the child but do not interfere. The child can direct the play, for example, 'You be the daddy. I am the mummy' or 'You make a ball with the clay,' and so on.

We may offer reflective statements of what we are observing, for example, 'You're using all the red bricks to build a high tower,' or about what we are hearing, 'You're telling me that in a minute you are going to knock the tower down.' We may reflect back emotion too, 'You're smiling and humming as you paint. You seem happy.'

Doing the above allows children to realise that you are interested in them, attentive and that you value what they are doing. This practice is based on the principles of person-centred counselling.

However, we have another role when supporting children's play, and that is to help children to extend their play. So if, for example, the child is playing at being a fire officer but is obviously struggling to know what to use for a hose, you could make some suggestions. Maybe roll up a piece of paper to make a hose or use the cardboard tube of a toilet roll. The key is to allow the child to choose. You are not leading but responding to the child's play and offering other materials and suggestions only.

When meeting a child alone, I usually have free play at the start of each session and sometimes at the end too, and occasionally my visit with the child will be what I term a 'play visit'. This is a free play session, usually for about 30 minutes. Children choose toys from a selection I bring along, or use their own. With those aged 12 and above, free play is probably an art and craft activity using materials as they please, or playing with a radio-controlled car, or a choice of board games.

When the child has had my full attention for 30 minutes I may then explain I need to speak to her mother/father/carer and so the next 30 minutes will be 'occupational play'. This means that the child may continue with the play activity she has been engaged in, but understands that I am no longer available to her. Sometimes with young or developmentally younger children it may be easier to provide a new play activity for the occupational play, as this creates an obvious distinction between the two types. The purpose is to occupy the child while the adults are busy. Once you have finished talking, you should spend a short time with the child so she can show and tell you what she has been doing.

Working this way gives you both a shared experience that you can look back on or talk about, creating positive memories and a history together. Positive experiences that meet needs can build resilience. If the child also talks positively to her parent/carer about her free play experience, it opens an opportunity for you to encourage the parent to do the same, supporting the child's development and enhancing both their lives. Play helps a child to cope with adversity by enriching life. Many of the patients I work with have impoverished experiences of play as children and I have found this can inhibit their willingness (and ability) to engage in play with their own children, missing out on opportunities for shared fun and relaxation. I try to help them see play in the same way as adults 'play', through their interests and hobbies and to recognise the hidden benefits of these activities, especially around mental health.

These are some examples of free play:

- Whenever possible I work in a playroom setting. I have set up a playroom in my office using one of the interview rooms (which other workers can use too), sourcing the toys from charity shops, car boot sales and so on. I could book a playroom in a child and family centre or school, but setting up and clearing away takes time, so from my perspective, it is only practical when I can see several children in a row and the time is justified.

  I ensure I include play materials that may be relevant to the children's lives, for instance, along with other play materials, a doctor's kit with a syringe and some tinfoil. Some years ago, when I worked in a child and family centre, a four-year-old put the baby doll in bed, collected the tin foil from the art area and the syringe from the doctor's kit and acted out the preparation of heroin, injecting the heroin and then its sleep-inducing effects. In the home area of the playroom another small child entered the play, 'You better no do that. If the social worker finds you, your bairn will get taken off you.' Both children's mothers were actively injecting heroin. Both thought they had concealed it from their children.

- I have set up my car as a play space. There are three big puppets on the back seat, a drawstring bag containing a variety of small toys, and I have made a garden (small world imaginative play) on the front dashboard. I also have four picture books and a scaling tool in the door pockets. Admittedly, I do have to clear the car for weekend shopping! In the boot of the car I keep my box of play activities and a travel rug, especially in summer, when we can extend our play space outside. The children love coming in the car. They will happily play away while we journey to the next venue. Clearly while driving I can offer very limited, if any, reflection, but I contribute when I can. Most children understand this, and the advantage of car travel is that it is a completely confidential space. Children often find the rhythm soothing and not being able to make eye contact a positive advantage, increasing their ability to feel safe.

- Visit a play park with children and they will use the equipment imaginatively.

- In the bag that I carry around with me I have pens, paper, finger puppets, cards, a bottle of bubbles, a story book, a small doll or teddy, some beads to thread, and I have been known to have mini pots of playdough. That gives me different choices of activities.

In conclusion, I encourage every worker to have free play with the children they work with to help build and maintain relationships.

Practice example

After using the *Traffic Lights* activity (see pp.72–75) with a nine-year-old one session (directed play), he expressed a wish that there was more time to play and asked if he could play with the bricks and dinosaurs, which we did for a further half hour. At the end he asked if I had any soldiers. I didn't, but got hold of some for the next free play session. He was waiting at the window for me and led me to the kitchen table. 'That's your side, Audrey.'

He then carefully set out the bricks at his side to make a building and chose the fiercest looking dinosaur and a set of red soldiers. He instructed me to make a building too and I was given blue soldiers and the more amenable-looking Diplodocus dinosaur, 'He's veggie so not much use for eating my soldiers.'

He attacked my building, knocking it clean down and killing my soldiers and dinosaur. He instructed me to build it back up again and defend myself, which I did, and he quickly annihilated me again. He was smiling now and definitely in charge. I joined the play, careful to follow his instructions whilst using my own imagination, for example, by making my soldiers take care of my dinosaur.

After about 15 minutes of repeating the same pattern he declared, 'We are going to make peace now. You've got to give me something. Your dinosaur will do and I'll give you some of my gold.'

We exchanged gifts and our camps joined. We were now a formidable fighting force ready to take on some of his action figures, fished out of the cupboard.

Ten minutes before the end I gave my usual time warnings. As we tidied up he said, 'Know what? I used to hate you and so did my mum, but you are good really. I like you now.'

I am not a therapist, but would suggest that his play that day mirrored the struggle in our relationship. I had made some difficult decisions for him and had separated him from his mother and placed him in foster care. He hadn't had a choice in that, and while it was the right decision, it had highlighted a huge power imbalance. He had been angry and upset with me during that period. Maybe our free play and the opportunity to direct me and express his anger in play had, to some extent, addressed that imbalance.

Another example of the benefit of free play with a supportive adult

I worked with a little child barely older than a toddler, who would ask to go in the car. As I strapped her into the car seat she would find the doll and the bear puppet, and as soon as I started the engine she would enter a world of play where the bear continuously hit and shouted angrily at the doll. I learned that I could just drive for five minutes, then stop and sit in the back seat with her. I didn't interfere, just reflected what was happening. One day she said 'You help the doll.' I took the doll in my arms away from the bear and comforted it. The bear proceeded to hit, shout and swear at me. Placing the doll at my side, I said to the bear, 'I am not scared of you and I won't let you hurt me or the dolly.' The little girl looked at the bear and said, 'Bad bear, bad daddy hurts me.' I reflected back to her that she was telling me that the bear was bad and that daddy hurt her.

The toddler replied, 'Daddy bad. He hits me. He will hit you too.'

Me: 'Your daddy hits you and you're worried he will hit me too?'

Child: 'Daddy's strong, he hurted the policeman, he hurted granny, he hits me but he will hurted you too!'

Me: 'I think we need help to sort this muddle out and keep you safe I think we need to speak to a very strong and safe policeman. Okay?'

Child: 'Yes and I will tell him 'bout daddy hurting.'

Chapter 4

Basic Principles When Working with Children

Timing

When at all possible, take into account the timing of your visit. We can assume that for most children meeting a strange adult is not high on their list of really fun things to do, and is more likely to be an anxiety-provoking experience. They may also have picked up a sense that the meeting is serious (they may, for example, have told a worry to a teacher/carer, who has explained that someone will come and talk to them later). If the child then has to meet you at playtime or when the rest of the class/family are doing something fun, this could further disadvantage the start of your working relationship. It is also a catalyst for a child who is already anxious and perhaps finding it difficult to manage strong emotions to present negative acting-out behaviour. If this happens you may not be able to proceed or you may need to spend considerable time managing behaviour before being able to engage the child in conversation.

I tend to time my visit (if it is in school) just after playtime or lunchtime. Children are more likely to feel settled having had a period of free play and having had their basic physical needs met. Check that young children have had the opportunity to go to the toilet. When working with older children I sometimes try to find out the subject they *least* like and then meet with them during that time. The young person is usually pleased to leave that class, and it often gives a welcome respite for teaching staff if the child tends to act out (it is fairly standard for more challenging behaviour to manifest when a child is being asked to do something he finds hard or dislikes). A word of caution – this may be good for the first visit, but if visits are ongoing, I would not want the child to miss the same class each time.

Similarly, if you are visiting a family home or residential unit, try to avoid:

- mealtimes
- when the child's favourite television programme is on
- the night that the child usually goes to a favourite activity.

Time your visit in a way that won't interrupt the child's routine. If you can't do this, then acknowledge it and apologise, if possible giving a reason: 'I am sorry that I've had to come and see you at playtime –it's not very fair is it? [pause] You see you are very important and I really wanted to see you today, but the problem is it is the only time I could visit. If I come back to see you again, I will try very hard to make it a different time. Is that okay?' Children are usually very forgiving.

When working long term with children, ideally meet with them the same time each week, if you are able to arrange this. If this is not possible, make a commitment to meet them, say, always in a morning after break, or maybe work out a rota so they are not missing the same class each week. The message here is to give the children a sense of predictability and routine, which is often lacking in their lives. It also increases the likelihood that your visits will become less newsworthy to the other children who will become used to Dave's social worker's visit every Monday much the same way as Susan's speech therapist's visit on Tuesdays.

Get the inside story

Speak to someone who knows the child well before you meet him. You need to find out the child's normal presentation and how he usually reacts to strangers, as well as wider questions about the child to help inform your assessment.

Ask about specific fears. If the child is frightened of balloons then you don't want to play a game with balloons. Find out about things he finds difficult. If he struggles with writing, he may associate pens and paper with failure so, at least on initial contact, use a different medium. Likewise find out about special interests, strengths and likes, so you can focus on these. Class projects, if the child is enjoying them, can be good to use as a conversation topic. Find out if the child has done something particularly well that day/week to include in conversation, 'Your teacher told me you got a gold star for your reading. Wow! That's impressive.' For an older child, who will be aware you have spoken to his teacher and may be wondering what was said, 'Before I met you I spoke to your teacher and she thinks you have lots of good ideas and you are sometimes very helpful.'

Whatever you choose to say, it should be true and specific to the child with whom you are working. Children see through false praise so it has no value.

Location – think about where you are going to meet the child

Rooms have meanings. I often work in schools and it is not uncommon for the headteacher to offer me his room or the deputy head's room to work in. While I appreciate this offer, I usually decline. The headteacher is a powerful and important person in school and so his room is likely to be loaded with meaning for the child, and I have no idea whether that meaning is positive or negative. When I explain this, it is usually understood. If possible, I ask for two options, so that the child can choose. In the summer this could include an outside space. A room the child doesn't often visit is good because the associated memories are limited. Quite often I end up in the visiting services room. Perfect.

Doing regular home visits is essential to the assessment process but I prefer not to meet children in their own home to do individual focused work. I need to work with a child in a confidential, safe space, and normal family life usually means access is granted to all members to most rooms without the courtesy of a warning knock. This means the child will not have the confidence he will not be interrupted when working with me.

In general, I avoid spending time in a child's bedroom, although I will visit briefly to admire a bedroom, if invited. Apart from issues of safety for the worker and the child, the bedroom should be the place where the child can relax and go to sleep. Bringing difficult or emotive subjects into a bedroom may create unwanted or upsetting associations. In addition, there could be issues for some children around abuse, particularly sexual abuse, which may have occurred in a bedroom. In considering safe caring, I would be cautious about being alone with a child in his bedroom, especially when we don't know each other very well. It is a very personal space and you must always be aware of the power imbalance in your relationship. To children, adults are very powerful, both in terms of size and strength, as well as in their authority to make decisions for children, and they may have experienced an adult's abuse of power in their lives. If I am with a child in his room I tend to sit on the floor beside the bed, close to the child but not in a physically powerful position, and leave the door ajar.

Perhaps the most neutral place to meet a child is in your workplace/office, if that is available to you. But be aware of possible problems with this. Children who have been abused may well have no reason to trust adults and may also have been given negative information about adults working with them, particularly social workers. For those children, if you take them away from a familiar setting, it may well cause stress (and remember, a child's stress is not always obvious to an adult). It is not uncommon for children to be told or threatened with being taken away from their families to bad places by social workers. Children have told me that they were afraid I would take them to 'Maggie Murphy's'. (Maggie Murphy is a character akin to a witch, who makes them wear 'jaggy jumpers'.)

However, once a child has a relationship with you it can be really important for him to visit your office, to know where you sit so he has a picture in his head of your world. I always put the pictures the child gives me up on the wall beside my desk, and the children love to see them. Sometimes a child needs to check all the rooms in a building before feeling safe (he may fantasise about what happens in the other rooms or around the corner), and this can be impractical in a busy office during the working day.

To deal with the issue of the unfamiliar building and the child's possible need to check out all the rooms, I always make my first visit to the centre at around 5.30pm, when the office is quiet and there are no telephone calls coming in. Then we can have a peek in all the rooms, if that helps the child to feel safe. A trip to your office, once the child knows you, can strengthen your relationship. I asked a young child who was about to turn six what she would like to do for a birthday outing with me. I suggested a picnic in the park, a trip to a city farm or soft play. She refused all of these and asked to, 'Go and sit at your desk, make a picture and put it on your wall and have a drink from the funny water machine.'

Prior to bringing the child to the office, I will usually have met him in school on his own and at home with his family. Thus the child will have some familiarity with me and hopefully this will reduce any potential anxiety. It is also important to remember that children can be very literal thinkers, so if they have not seen you in their home and you are picking them up from school, they may fear you do not know how to find their home to return them safely there after the session. They may be preoccupied by worries about how they will get home. Often children we work with are used to taking care of themselves, and don't feel reassured that the adult knows what to do, especially if you are still a stranger to them. This is why it is important to talk about the plan in advance, remind them of it and be able to demonstrate that you are capable of following it through:

> 'I will collect you from school. Your teacher will wait with you at reception. We will go to the [social work centre] to do some activities and then I will take you home in my car. I wonder if I will be able to park in the same space as last time when we get to your house?'

Prepare the person who is going to bring the child to you

There are several reasons why I prefer somebody the child knows and feels comfortable with to bring the child to me:

- It gives the child some sense of safety or familiarity. Being taken somewhere, even to a familiar room, to an adult you don't know, can feel unsafe and frightening, particularly to young children who may be experiencing abuse by a person more powerful than them.

- It provides me with the opportunity to demonstrate to the child that I approve of his safe adult and that the safe adult trusts me. Children and indeed adults often warm to, and feel more positive about, strangers if someone they know and trust recommends that person. As adults we listen to the opinion of friends about a new person joining a group. Similarly, young children watch their parents/safe adult closely for cues that a stranger is safe, the cues showing in the interaction with the new person.

    When the safe adult leaves I usually try to reinforce that I liked him by offering a compliment, for example, 'I really liked your teacher's jumper. It was a lovely colour.'

- Lastly, it gives me time to set up the room and position myself so that I am not towering over the child when he comes in.

Bearing all this in mind, it is obviously important to prepare the trusted person as to how you will work and what you want him to do or not do.

- First check out that he is indeed the person whom the child would feel most comfortable with and not just the nearest person to hand or the designated child protection person. I explain why I need someone who knows the child well, and find that other professionals are very understanding and willing to accommodate my request.

- Ask that the trusted person checks with the child if he needs to visit the toilet before he comes to see you. With young children (under seven) they should be encouraged to 'go and try'. Make sure that you also know where the toilets are and if the child can manage independently.

- Make sure you know where the child is to be returned to after the interview. Does the child know how to get there or do you need to know where to take him?

- When you are planning the interview with the support staff, discuss what explanation to give the child for the meeting. Use simple words and terminology. This applies to children of any age. First, you might think about not using your job title immediately. I am a social worker and know this can shut down communication before I have started as it is possible parents/other adults have threatened the child with social workers. Second, it is a job title and it doesn't really tell the child anything about what you are going to do. The children we work with often have language delays, limited life experience and will almost certainly be feeling anxious. An introduction that includes the purpose of the visit, 'This is John. He is going to look at your sore finger and see if he can make it better,' is always more reassuring than, 'This is the doctor who will see you.' So I might introduce myself like this: 'My name is Audrey. I am a safe adult. I help children and the people who look after them with muddles and problems and help keep children safe.'

- Before they leave the room, make sure the trusted adult tells the child in your presence where he will be while the child is with you. This ensures the child will know that the trusted adult is still accessible (and do check that the trusted adult *is* accessible to the child).

- Ask the trusted adult to demonstrate in an obvious way that he is comfortable around you. For example, if you have worked together before he might mention this in front of the child or talk about something you will be doing together in the future. Be aware of body language. Seeing you smile and chat socially for a few minutes can be very reassuring for the child, who is looking for clues about how safe you are.

- Explain to the trusted adult that you will be doing an activity when he arrives with the child and explain how you will initiate engagement and that it is a particular approach you use.

- Work out a signal between you to indicate that it is time for him to ask the child if he can leave, and explain that if the child does not give permission for him to leave he should not go. Explain what you will do next.

- And lastly, but perhaps most importantly, ask the trusted adult to ensure that you are not interrupted. On one (rare) occasion in a school, within a period of 30 minutes, six people had walked into the room unannounced. On one of the occasions the little boy had begun saying, 'My dad...' when the door opened and he completely closed down. Earlier that day he had been heard saying to a friend that his dad hit him and it was sore. Two weeks later he was removed from home when his siblings disclosed serious physical abuse. Arguably, he was at home for two weeks longer than he should have been because of interruptions.

Set up the room before the child arrives

Try to make the room into your own space. I set out some of my games or activities beforehand. I also usually bring the same teddy bear each time. For younger children it is 'Big Ted' with long arms that give hugs easily, but when working with older children whose emotional development is age appropriate, I use 'Little Ted', a miniature teddy bear. He can sit less obviously beside my diary or on top of my bag, and if they want to borrow him he fits in a pocket to take away.

Think about where the chairs are in a room. You don't want to hem a child in. Try and allow the child the option to sit near the door and be careful you are not blocking his exit. Remember that the child may feel afraid of you. Always try to be sitting when the child comes in. If at all possible sit lower than the child to make yourself appear less threatening.

Think about what you are going to be doing when the child arrives. Always be engaged in an activity that centres on play. If I have learned that a child loves dogs but I don't have any dog toys or tools with me, I will get felt tips and paper out and be drawing dogs when the child arrives. This is important because it makes you immediately interesting; the child wonders what you are doing or wants to do the same. It provides an icebreaker, something to talk about instantly, before introductions.

Adult manners dictate introductions before conversation, but children don't operate that way. They will approach other children by starting out with a comment about what that child is doing or asking to have a turn of the other child's toy. It is only a little later that they will tell each other their names. We can mimic this.

On the day I was drawing dogs (having been told the little boy liked dogs) I carried on with my drawing for just a few seconds after the boy entered the room to allow him to observe me before I made eye contact with him. Again this mimics how children behave. They will watch another child first before they approach. Then I looked up, said 'Hi', making *brief* eye contact (eye contact can be threatening) while holding my picture up. I then said, deliberately imitating children's language, 'I am drawing dogs. Want to play?'

The child responded by letting go of his teacher's hand and coming and sitting next to me. Again it is important to try to give the child a sense of control over the decision to stay. If he had said no, I would simply have carried on drawing and talking, trying to engage him. Then at a later point, maybe 5–10 minutes later, I would have asked him to come and help me, maybe to get something else out of my bag or to cut out the drawing or perhaps saying I wanted to play a game that needed two people.

In this case I gave the boy some paper and offered him my pens and he began to draw. It was only after admiring his picture that I introduced myself, his teacher still in the room. 'My name is Audrey. My job is to try and help children to keep safe and your teacher asked me to come and see you 'cos she is worried about you.' You should pause to let the child take this in, as a child's brain takes nearly twice as long as an adult's to process the spoken word.

'See, I am going to show you my badge. It's got a photo on it that I think makes me look silly!' After looking at the I.D. badge I went back to the drawing. This gave the child thinking space. A few minutes later I nodded to the teacher for her to ask the child if it was okay for her to leave.

Offer a nurturing experience at the start of your interview

A significant number of the children I meet will, to some extent, be experiencing neglect. I tend to offer them a drink and a small snack at the start. It's not difficult to carry a small carton of fruit juice and a little box of raisins or a satsuma in your bag. If the child is hungry this will meet a basic physical need and should help to improve the child's concentration. It is also nice to share the snack with the child – eating together, in most cultures, is a significant positive and familiar activity. Likewise, if the child is cold, move closer to the radiator or slip your coat around him. As well as offering the child basic nurturing as you would with any child, it also demonstrates that you care about him and can meet at least some of his needs.

For some children this is a very powerful message. I worked with one little girl who constantly had head lice and she was clearly very uncomfortable. The second time I met her I came prepared with a head lice comb, cotton wool and a plastic bag. We took 10 minutes at the start of the meeting to rid her of the worst of the lice. She was a different girl after that. Her concentration improved and her willingness to engage increased. Not everyone will be comfortable doing this, but as a former nursery nurse I am used to dealing with head lice. Also, *and I stress this*, the girl was 12 years old and able to consent to me doing this for her, and I also informed the parent of the head lice after my first meeting and gained her permission to comb through her child's hair if the child agreed.

Give the child an exit strategy

At the start of the interview tell the child he can leave if he wants to, but the rule is he needs to go straight back to class (or to the person he arrived with). Explain that you need to know he is safe so you would have to go with him.

You may want to work out with a child what he would say if he wanted to stop the session. I tend to use the phrase 'Stop the bus.' To date, none of the children I have worked with have chosen to end the session early, but it is important to give them that option. If they know they *can* leave, they are more likely to relax.

Chapter 5

The Child

Stage, not age

This is so important, I cannot emphasise it enough.

We all know children go through stages in each area of their development. There is an order to the developmental stages and theorists give us a guide to which stage should be reached at which age. Failing to meet a developmental milestone is seen as an indicator of a *possible* problem that is either intrinsic to the child (a learning difficulty or health issue) or may be an indicator that the child is not having her needs adequately met in order to grow and develop at the expected rate. Sustained physical or emotional neglect will almost certainly impede a child's development.

Most of the children I work with have fragmented development. That is to say, some areas of their development would be considered to be age appropriate, but other areas are more at the stage of a younger child. Typically, they are developmentally younger than their chronological age in areas of language, and social and emotional development.

For these children this can be a real problem in their day-to-day lives. A big strapping lad of 14, outwardly keeping up with peer group trends, is expected by adults to *act* like a 14 year old. But he doesn't, and this is too easily read as being immature or deliberately disobedient. Too often such children attract labels such as 'conduct disorder'.

The same applies for the four-and-a-half-year-old who begins school where there are expectations that she will be able to listen to and follow simple instructions and understand the notion of taking turns in play. Most of the four- to five-year-olds I work with have not yet learned this.

For children like these, fragmented development (and for some there may be global developmental delay and almost certainly issues around attachment) due to unmet needs at critical developmental stages has left them without the capacity to do the tasks demanded of their age group.

'Not had their needs met' is a common phrase in assessments, both verbal and written. It is worth taking a moment to reflect on how serious an issue this is, and the enormity of the disadvantage faced by the child when needs are not met adequately, to the point where development is delayed. Think how it feels to constantly fail because the adults and peers around you expect more of you than you are capable of. How cruel the world is for a child in that position. Some may have their needs met in one area of their lives but not another, and in this case, the one positive area can be a resilience factor for the child. Sadly many of the children I work with do not have their needs met at home or at school or in their communities. *But* as adults working with these vulnerable children, we can meet them at their developmental stage (and encourage others to do this also). We can offer them a relationship that gives them what they need. We can provide opportunities that are appropriate to their developmental stage, not age, especially through play and activities.

This was brought home to me during one of my first shifts as a residential officer. The children in my care that day were all teenagers and I had not worked with teenagers before. Now I was faced with a group of six, unknown to me, except I had been told that the group was very unsettled and there had been some challenging behaviour. As I began my shift, a fire alarm went off and a group of excitable teenagers ran past me. My colleague calmly replaced the broken glass on the fire alarm box and told me this was a common occurrence.

By then the butterflies in my stomach had turned into flapping dragons. The stampeding teenagers rushed past again and I tried to stop them as I would have done with the toddlers I was used to looking after, by raising my hand and saying firmly, 'Stop running!' They did stop, briefly, but before I could finish asking if they wanted to go outside and play football, they were off again.

Feeling very out of my depth, I realised there was no way I was going to gain authority over the group. They didn't know me and had no relationship with me at that point. I knew I somehow needed to engage them before I could hope to gain control and I needed something unusual with high entertainment value. Because the behaviour I observed was reminiscent of excited, out-of-control toddlers, first I tried distracting them by offering a snack and a drink. Nurturing and feeding often settles small children. As they whizzed passed the kitchen I playfully shouted, 'Juice and biscuits for sale.' This worked to some degree, and thankfully four out of the six joined me.

This wasn't going to hold them for long, however. Wracking my brain for what to do next and unable to see any basic play materials around (I later found games locked in a cupboard), I suddenly struck upon glup. This is cornflour and water mixed together which makes a smooth textured play material – messy, but with the advantage of brushing off clothes when dry. (See Appendix I for the recipe.)

So, with pots and basins, cornflour and water, I went through to the dining room, calling, 'Come and see' when asked what I was doing. One or two followed to watch me mix the cornflour and water and in a playful voice I shouted, 'I've got slime!'

Two teenagers dived in. I encouraged squealing, laughing and general noise, and within 10 minutes all six had joined in and were covered from head to toe in glup. Yes it was noisy, yes it was mayhem, with glup going everywhere, but it was play.

Observing them I could see that it was mostly solitary or parallel play, reminiscent of much younger children. They were happy and gradually relaxed and chatted to me and at the end, when asked, helped with the tidy up time. I now began to feel at home and believe I *could* work with teenagers, and I was beginning to love it.

The point I want to make here is that if you hit the right stage of development, your engagement will work, be meaningful and possibly therapeutic. Hit the wrong stage and the child will disengage quickly, and the possibility of confrontation over minor issues is more likely. The teenagers didn't know me but I was able to establish rapport fairly quickly through providing play and within that, care and nurture. It was also important that I was able to contain the children so they felt safe with me. They had tested the boundaries and knew how far they could go. Of course they had to do this repeatedly and in different situations before they felt contained by me.

When choosing an activity from this book think about developmental stage, not age. I worked with a teenage boy using the *Traffic Lights* activity (see pp.72–75). He engaged with it initially by agreeing to 'test it out' for me, but then requested it again and again. While it was directed play, because we were talking about his behaviour and offending through it, it also legitimised his enjoyment of playing with cars.

One of my older girls (13) responded well to using a storybook and puppets. My observations of her presentation helped me to assess her as being six to eight years old in her emotional development, but she was aware that most 13-year-olds would have viewed the story as being 'for babies'. So to help her to engage with it, I asked her to help me to test it before I used it with younger children. She readily agreed, enjoyed it and decided she needed to test other activities to make sure *they* would work.

Even if nothing else was achieved, this allowed me to give her play experiences she had either missed or needed to revisit, which is so valuable in healing, and helped our relationship. We had common ground. We were both helpers and we both enjoyed play.

When children trust you enough to tell you a worry, they expect action

When children take a leap of faith and trust you enough to tell you a worry or disclose abuse or neglect, they need comfort, concern and care, *but they also want action.*

Children are wiser than they are sometimes given credit for. They know we do not carry magic wands and can't fix things that are going wrong overnight, but if they tell us what the matter is, they do it because they seek change. Perhaps it has all got too much and they may be desperate.

As a worker you could be in a tricky position here. Internally you may be thinking, 'This is the evidence I need to help make things better' but *you* know it will be in the future and there is not much you can do now. The problem is that the child wants to see something change now. Ultimately, no one can stop a bully overnight or stop a parent using drugs today, or find a lost puppy in the next hour. But if we are to retain our credibility in the eyes of the child we must find an action after the disclosure and we must also be honest with the child.

The skill here is to look for the often very small but significant things you can do and be honest about what you can't do or what will take time to do.

For example, in response to a disclosure of bullying and after showing concern, care and empathy:

> 'You and I both know that I can't stop Scott bullying you. But I think that together we can work out how you can keep yourself safer. Let's do the shield activity again and see if we can put more things in.'

Or, with mum on drugs again:

> 'So mum has taken drugs again. I can't stop her doing that and nor can you. Mum is making a choice, but we can keep you safe while mum is doing drugs. I think we will speak to nana and see if you can go and stay there.'

Or for the lost puppy:

> 'I will look out for your puppy while I am doing visits but I also think you could make a quick poster and I'll put it up where the other social workers can see it and they will look too. You could make another one too and I will drop that off at the police station, okay?'

And for the neglected child:

> 'You're telling me that you can't find any clean pants and socks at home and other children call you smelly. Well, let's see if we can organise for you to have a little wash in the teacher's bathroom before school starts and I will go and get you some new pants and socks.'

How to handle loyalty

It is not an uncommon experience to find children who have been badly hurt by a parent remaining completely loyal to the parent. This may be explained by a complex and often harmful attachment history and/or a fear aroused by threats of punishment if the child should tell. This places the child who needs help in a very difficult position. How does a child tell another adult that a parent is hurting or frightening her when the child believes this will lead to criticism or even trouble for that parent (or the fear of being taken away)?

Children who are abused are frequently told things like:

'If you tell the social worker you will get taken away.'

'If you tell, the police will come and get me and I won't speak to you again.'

'If you tell, bad people will take me away and who will look after you then?'

So it is important that we convey to children that we have respect for a parent and that we understand that the parent has good parts as well as not-so-good parts. In this way we give the child permission to acknowledge a parent's failings or bad parts, with the understanding that we (the worker) will not see the parent as all bad. There are parallels here to working with domestic violence. Abused partners will return again and again to violent partners because they state they love them. In my experience the victims will often disengage with agencies/workers who convey the message that all they can see is the partner's bad or dangerous behaviour.

I worked with a family with three children. The father was the main carer in the family home. He did the bedtime routines, helped make tea and so on. He was also the more energised and responsive parent and contributed in no small way to meeting the children's needs.

In response to a referral from a member of the public who said they had witnessed the father assaulting the oldest child (age nine), a police officer and I went out to interview the child in school.

The child already knew me and I had a good relationship with her. However, on being brought to meet me, she was exceptionally quiet, despite being normally quite bubbly, and she refused to talk about her day.

I took a story out of my bag, *Mog on Fox Night* – it pays to know your children's stories – in which an essentially good father gets angry (Kerr 1993). At that point in the story I stopped and said, 'All dads get angry sometimes don't they?' She nodded her head vigorously. At a later point in the story, where the father was being more positive, I said, 'And all dads have good parts too, don't they?'

Again, lots of nodding. Then I asked, 'Is that like your daddy too? Does he have lots of good parts but sometimes an angry part too?' She replied firmly and clearly, 'Yes.'

I then asked if she could tell us what happened today on the way to school and she told us about her father assaulting her.

After the interview she asked what would happen to her father. I explained we needed to help him to manage his behaviour. It wasn't okay for him to hurt her, no matter how angry he felt. I then asked what would happen if she hit the other children in the playground, and she said she would get into trouble and if it was 'a big hit' she might not be allowed out next playtime.

I explained that it would be the same for her father. He would get a row and he might have to miss out of free time for a bit because he had given a big hit to a little girl.

She completely accepted the explanation and on further discussion it was clear she viewed it as fair. Even more reassuring was the fact that she had grasped that sometimes having a consequence to an action was helpful.

Some time later, this little girl was able to tell me about earlier domestic abuse.

Building trust

When you are likely to be working with a child for more than just a one-off session, make it your mission to prove that you are consistent and reliable. I tell children (who are developmentally able to understand), 'I will always keep my promises. If I say I will bring my good pens next week, I will. If I tell you that if you don't stop swinging on your chair I will be cross, then that will happen.'

It is very important that you don't make promises you can't keep. A good way to show that you are reliable and consistent is to set up situations to demonstrate this. At the end of a session I might tell a child that I will send her a postcard, and I do it. I keep a folder of postcards in my office drawer and as soon as I return to my office, I write a quick greeting and put it through the system to be posted.

Similarly, the promise to bring my good pens or a puppet is noted in my diary beside the child's next appointment. As a matter of habit I keep most of the things I use in the office or in the boot of my car, so I don't forget to bring them from home. You will find your own strategies to ensure you remember to follow through. To forget to fulfil a promise will only confirm to a child who has just met you that you are yet another adult who can't be trusted. For the child who is slowly beginning to trust, it can be distressing and potentially set back the development of your relationship.

Vulnerable children need to see multiple demonstrations of your reliability, care and commitment to them. If you can do this it will give them a reason to invest in a relationship with you or strengthen your existing relationship. Once a meaningful relationship is established you may not need to do it as often, but don't stop altogether as most vulnerable children need to be reminded on a regular basis. They are often coping with more than we know. Their focus is on survival, and if this is the case, it will likely have an impact on their ability to process and retain information. It is therefore understandable that they need frequent repetition of reassuring routines and reminders that we are consistent caring adults who can be relied upon.

Chapter 6

Using Self and the Environment

Managing a professional relationship with a child

Do not underestimate the impact you will have on some children. In successfully building a relationship with a child, you are taking on huge responsibilities to:

- hold, or emotionally contain, the child safely in the relationship

- maintain the boundaries and help the child find and develop other relationships

- end the relationship when the time comes in a sensitive and positive way; it may be the first good ending the child has had.

You will hopefully have established a regular contact pattern with the child. It should be predictable and provide the child with a small oasis of relative calm in his daily life. Even the most challenging sessions with a caring, safe adult can still bring some respite for a child whose world is full of chaos and unpredictability.

What happens when the routine is disrupted, by going on holiday, for instance? Some of the children will be neither up nor down about the break. You will have prepared them beforehand and they will accept it and have faith that you will return. But for others it can be stressful. To alleviate this, a powerful tool is the use of transitional objects. My elf puppet, which travels in the back of the car with me, has spent a number of holidays with children while I am away. As he is very popular with children who expect to find him in my car, I have a twin in case anything happens to him and he doesn't return. I also have a small teddy bear, 'Little Ted', which does the same.

All of the children I work with receive a postcard while I am away on holiday. However, I do not think about work while I am on holiday – we have a responsibility to keep ourselves emotionally well, and a complete break is essential at least once a year. So I write my postcards before I go. The children don't know where I am going on holiday, so over the year I collect postcards of seaside scenes or just pictures which will attract a child (dogs, cats, toys, etc.) and in advance of my holiday I write a little message (two or three lines maximum) to each child and leave them with a colleague to be posted half-way through my break.

Allow children to dip in and out of a conversation

There is a real skill in this, but with thought and practice it can be achieved and will eventually become second nature.

When children are talking about things that are important to them or perhaps about difficult and upsetting subjects, they can find that the conversation becomes too intense and so they change the subject or focus onto another activity and switch off the adult. Most of us can remember doing this as a child, especially when being told off, and as often as not hearing, 'Stop changing the subject,' or 'Are you listening to me?'

I am not often in the position of needing to tell a child off, but I do frequently need to talk about sensitive and difficult issues. Sometimes, due to the nature of my work, I have to introduce the subject. I will have done this through one of the activities in this book, but nonetheless the conversation has been instigated by me and is therefore not child-led. This can be stressful for a child, so he will change the subject or disengage from the conversation. I find the use of an activity lessens the frequency of this happening, but it may still occur.

Another situation when this happens is when a child begins to tell you something (to disclose) and then panics and feels he has told you too much and so actively disengages or changes focus.

The essential thing to remember is that this is a coping mechanism, a safety valve if you like, so we must not try to stop it. The child is protecting himself emotionally. It is our job to support, nurture and engage children. If we interfere with their coping mechanisms we are becoming unsafe adults because we are pushing them to do something that they are trying to protect themselves from. So what do you do when you are faced with a situation where you need to explore a serious issue and you feel that if you could just get a little more information, you could really help the child?

The answer is, go with the child. Be child-centred and let the child change the subject. Focus on the activity and join in with him. But acknowledge what is happening. So, I would perhaps say,

> 'It's really hard to talk about that stuff and it is okay to have a break for a while, so you have decided that we are going to talk about [your haircut]. Maybe we can talk about it again in a wee while?'

Or for a younger child:

> 'Okay, we are going to play with Lego bricks now. You don't want to talk [about mummy] for a wee while.'

What you have done is reflected back what the child is doing (talking about a haircut), acknowledged that the other subject is difficult and raised the expectation that we will come back to the subject. Ideally, I would not want to raise a difficult subject until the child did, but there are occasions when we have no choice, for instance, when there is the risk of immediate danger to the child and the conversation you are having is part of your assessment and will influence the next actions you take.

Try to give the child as much time as possible to continue to play and talk and hopefully bring up the issue by himself, before you raise the subject again. If you do need to instigate the conversation, be sensitive. Give the child an honest and truthful reason why you need to talk about it, appropriate to his developmental stage.

'When we were talking about mummy I felt that there were some scary or worried feelings around.' Pause, to give the child time to assimilate this. You might then ask if you are right and offer other suggestions if told you are wrong. 'Maybe it was upset or angry feelings? Can you be brave and tell me more about mummy and help me to understand because I would like to try and help? I care about you.'

I might try owning the feelings as my own. 'When you said mummy shouted I wondered if you were scared 'cos when I was a little girl I got scared when grown ups shouted.' This gives another opening into fuller conversation.

Take time and try to limit direct eye contact and use a soft tone of voice. Don't ask the child to look at you, and in almost all cases I would suggest you don't stop the activity the child is engaged in, but rather keep him doing it.

Practice example

The following is based on a real case but the details have been changed.

The child had been talking about her mother's 'silly' behaviour. She raised this spontaneously while we were playing with the doll's house. She stopped mid-conversation, dropped the dolls and moved to my bag, pulled out the playdough and asked to use it.

I said, 'Okay. Time for a wee break from playing with the house and talking about mummy. You would like to use the playdough now. Let's set it up.'

Meanwhile I was thinking I really needed to know more about this 'silly' behaviour. It sounded like the mother might be using drugs again.

The child enthusiastically got the playdough out and began to play with it in a general way, excluding me from her play. I joined in and invited her to direct me on one or two occasions and asked her to show me how to make a replica of her model. This was done deliberately. I wanted to empower her and give her a sense of control. She played happily but after 30 minutes there was no sign of her returning to talk about her mother or to play with the doll's house and I was concerned enough to need to explore it further.

Therefore I began to lead the play. I made some currant buns out of my playdough and together we sang and played 'Five Currant Buns in the Baker's Shop'. I introduced her mother back into our world by singing, 'Along came mummy with a penny one day, bought a currant bun and took it right away.'

When the song was finished I asked 'Does mummy like currant buns?' She laughed and shook her head. We played in silence for a few minutes. I was hoping she would spontaneously return to tell me about her mother's 'silly' behaviour, but she didn't.

I decided I was going to have to lead and be more direct. I took my elf puppet out of my bag and the child was immediately curious. I explained that I needed to talk to elf for a minute because I had a worry, a problem. Maybe she could help elf work out what I should do.

'Oh, Mr Elf, Emma was playing with the dolls a wee while ago and she told me mummy's silly behaviour had come back. I am here to keep Emma safe and to try to help her mummy too and I am really worried that mummy might be taking bad medicine again. I want to ask Emma more about mummy's silly behaviour. Emma's very brave you know but I don't want to upset her or make her feel afraid. What do you think I should do?'

'What's that, elf? You want to ask Emma?' I handed the elf to Emma.

'Just ask me about that stuff', she proclaimed.

So I said, 'Emma, tell me more about mummy's silly behaviour.'

Emma described the behaviour and said she also thought her mother was taking bad medicine again because the man with the red cap and gold car was back. She went on to say she had had lots of 'chippy teas' and had been going to her gran's before school because her gran gave her toast. Emma had been getting herself ready for school.

With older children, if giving them time and then introducing the subject of their mother subtly into the conversation did not work, I might move to a more direct approach, and as sensitively as possible, say something like:

> 'I thought you were very brave earlier when you were talking about mum. You know I am here to keep you safe and try to help you, but also to help mum. Can you tell me a bit more about what you were saying earlier? Do you remember you were talking about the man with the gold car being mum's friend again?'

If children don't take these opportunities, it is very important not to push further. It will only close communication down and damage your relationship. But it is equally important that they know they still have your approval and that you are not upset with them. They will tell you when they can.

You might comment:

'I'm sorry I am asking you to tell me more and maybe you can't just now. It's okay. I needed to ask you because I care about you and I am worried.'

At this point I would pause. Older children will often be able to tell you now what is going on. If not:

'But I trust you. I know you will help me understand when you can. Or maybe you could tell someone else, one of your other safe adults like your [key worker/teacher/ youth worker].'

At this point I may try the *Safe Hands* activity or *Beads and Badges* or *Candle Work* (see pp.125–127, pp.119–21 and pp.187–90 respectively).

I would also offer a nurturing response in the form of a drink or helping the child on with his coat or give teddy a hug to give him.

At the end of the session I would offer a transitional object (see p. 45) some fun interaction and also ensure the child knew when he would see me again. I would try to make that soon, even if very briefly. As a follow-up I would alert the child's other safe adults to the fact that he may have a worry or may have been trying to disclose. I would make it clear that I did not expect them to ask the child about this, but ensure that in the coming days they would try to have even brief periods of one-to-one time with the child. Maybe the child could be asked to help the teacher wash the paint brushes at the end of the day, or in a residential setting have some special time out with the key worker, where they couldn't be interrupted.

Work in a variety of settings

I have already discussed the importance of choosing the right location when working with children to ensure safety and security. In order to complete an accurate and comprehensive assessment, I also believe it is important to try to meet the child in a variety of settings and also to see him on his own *and* with different combinations of family members for example, the child with his parents and siblings; the child and his siblings; the child and his grandparent or significant other family member. When possible I also like to observe the child in his peer group, perhaps in the playground or at a children's club. It is usually possible to find an unobtrusive way of doing this, particularly with nursery and primary schoolchildren. With teenagers it can be hard to observe them with peers and I won't do it unless I can find a way that is not uncomfortable for the young person.

In all these situations, unless it is a purely observational visit, you can use play and playfulness as a vehicle to communication. When I am not doing a focused piece of work with a child, for instance when my primary purpose is to meet the parents, or on a car journey or waiting for a medical to take place, I always have something in my bag or in the car to entertain or initiate conversation because:

- It works. It gives the message that I am child friendly, and shared experiences and fun help build relationships.

- In some situations when children are distressed they need to be distracted. In addition, play can be a medium through which care and understanding can be offered in a way they are familiar with.

So, get ready to be able to play wherever you are. You don't need a lot of toys. Playing peek-a-boo, telling a joke, singing a silly song, playing I-spy or Granny went Shopping are all play and we can do that no matter where.

However, I happen to like toys and so do an awful lot of adults and children, so equip your bag (a canvas bag with lots of pockets is ideal) and get your car kitted out. If you have fun you can be sure the children you work with will too.

Make it your own

Most of the activities in this book have been made in response to a particular child's need and/or my need to talk to the child about a particular issue. *Traffic Lights* was developed for a boy of eight who loved cars. I adapted it for use with a radio-controlled car for a teenage boy, who loved it just as much.

One of the foster carers I trained recognised that this activity would be useful for a child in her care, but the child wasn't interested in cars but *was* interested in racehorses. So cars were exchanged for racehorses, parking spaces for stables and instead of traffic lights she used 3, 2, 1 and a whistle. This is exactly what you need to do. Adapt the ideas to the individual child, who will enjoy them so much more if the activity incorporates his interests. Don't be afraid to try new ideas.

When training, people ask me how I do this and where the ideas come from. I am naturally creative and I have worked with children for a long time and have learned so much from them. I have also had the benefit of working with so many talented people, including nursery nurses, psychotherapists, social workers and psychologists. But I have also benefited from working with students and newly qualified workers who are perhaps less experienced and often nervous but full of enthusiasm, optimism and a willingness to learn and try out new things. This always benefits the children and helps maintain my energy too.

To show you the process involved in creating a specific activity, I have compiled a fictitious case example based on years of experience:

Practice example

A boy of 12 damaged property in the garden of another child. This child's parent went to the boy's door and demanded that he be brought to the door to answer for his actions.

On a routine visit to the family the following day, I saw the child with some of the worst multiple injuries I have seen inflicted on a child. I took him to the hospital and once he had been treated, a forensic interview took place when he very coherently described the assault, but was not able to talk about the damage to the garden and property.

As his social worker I was puzzled, as he was not a child I would expect to have caused damage. It was out of character and I wanted to find out more about this and yet I knew he was not able to talk about it at this point, so what should I do?

I asked the police for more details and they told me he was with a friend and described the damage done to toys. Direct questioning about the damage was, I suspect, not going to work so I had to find another way to communicate. First, I thought about his developmental *stage* and concluded he was operating at a younger stage than 12 years. I recalled from previous visits that he had enjoyed storytelling and that he had been very enthusiastic when I drew him pictures. So I prepared for the next time I would see him by drawing and laminating pictures representing the child, a friend, the garden, the toys that were damaged, the woman who assaulted him, his mother, the police officer and me. Before you think I must be a great artist, I am really not that good, but I highlighted features like the shoes I wear, my beaded watch, the child's favourite cap or football shirt, *and* you can always put the names on the figures.

I took these with me to the next session and after some free play, I brought out a folder containing these figures and some spare card and pens. I explained that there were many kinds of stories – fairy tales, adventure stories and true stories. Sometimes stories were told with words, sometimes with pictures and if you were lucky, with both words and pictures. Today we were going to tell a true story and I had made some pictures to help. I pulled out the first picture, of me, and asked if he could guess who it was. He laughed and said, 'It's you.' I told him not to laugh too much because guess who was coming next? 'It's me,' he said. He was delighted with the pictures and spontaneously started playing with them, giving them voices. I then introduced the picture of the garden and the toys that were damaged and I asked: 'Can you tell me the true story of what happened?'

He acted out a series of events with the paper cut-outs and gave very specific details and voice intonation. He was spontaneous in his delivery and appeared to be showing me a real scene, thinking about where to place pictures and informing me of things I had missed. He showed me that he and his friend had been playing a game without malicious intent. He then went on to demonstrate what happened when he was assaulted, repeating what he had said in the forensic interview. This gave me the opportunity to discuss both parts of the event with him, as he had shown he was now able to talk about it.

What I always have in my bag

- Good quality felt-tip pens.

- A small picture storybook and joke book (because I can never remember jokes).

- Small drawing pad with blank paper.

- Picture dice (these can be bought in most good bookshops. They are dice with pictures instead of dots, and can be used to create stories around the picture revealed after a throw).

- Three finger puppets.

- A set of 'Getting to Know You' question cards (see Appendix II).

- A small teddy (key ring size) – I call him 'Little Ted'.

- A tube of fruit chews or packet of raisins and a small bottle of water.

- Tissues – for runny noses or alternatively, to make clothes for the puppets.

- Glittery self-adhesive stars and a selection of other stickers (to reward).

I have found the above (and a big bag) to be basic essentials that allow me to work spontaneously almost anywhere.

How to use your car

I have always had a teddy or two in my car. My 24-inch elf puppet lives on the back seat of my car and my dragon puppet often comes along for a ride. I am fortunate to have lots of nooks and crannies in my car and they will be stuffed with things like a *Feely Bag* (see pp.172–76), which satisfies all the five senses, a story book or two and a fleece blanket. Lots of children like to wrap the fleece around them, if offered.

In the boot of the car I have a picnic bag (the insulated type) in which I keep some bottles of water or juice and some healthy snacks. Also in the boot, I keep a travel rug and baby wipes. In the summer I also have sand buckets, big household paintbrushes and a larger container of water. I use this to do water painting, perhaps on the pavement outside a child's house or in a park. I first saw this play when I was a nursery nurse. You fill your bucket with water and the child dips the brush in and then paints the water onto the tarmac or paving slabs to make pictures, which disappear as the sun dries them up. This fascinates young children and older children love to engage in 'water graffiti'.

But what most children like about my car is the garden I have on my dashboard. To be honest, the first time I made a garden in my car, it was not for working with children but purely being good to me. I love the countryside and hate having to live and work in the city, and wanted to keep a little bit of the countryside with me. This will not be for everyone, but I have an old car so I didn't mind using silicon glue to attach moss, stones, driftwood, acorns, fir cones and so on onto my dashboard. I added a little dish with a wet sponge in it to hold a few fresh flowers and at moments in my day I could take comfort from my little bit of countryside.

Then I found that parents and children really liked it. They touched it, asked questions, brought things to add to it and there are times when it has almost become a community garden. When I asked a girl of 13 what she would like if she attended school all week, she said 'To help tidy and make your garden.'

She did attend school and as a reward she was presented with a clean dashboard and a new tube of silicon glue, and she designed a garden from scratch. We took photographs and her mother and gran had to come and visit.

Over the years I have added little elves and fairies occasionally or semi-precious stones to wish on, and have begun to use it in different ways. Cars in themselves are good third objects. A short drive in the car and then relaxing with a drink and a snack while using the dashboard garden has been very popular with the children. I might ask where they would like to sit in the garden. 'If you could magically shrink, which special people would you bring to visit you in the garden? What wish would you make with the wishing stone? The little elf is holding a message (or question) for you. Can you point to the acorn that is feeling the way you are today?' (I have painted emotion faces on the acorns.)

If you pull down the sun visor in my car you will see little posters that give positive messages like, 'Be kind' or 'It's okay to tell' or 'You are great'. These are made of little bits of laminated card, attached with Velcro strips. Sometimes I make it personal and you can imagine the delighted smiles when I ask a child to pull down the visor and they see 'Happy Birthday, Mary' written there. I have a supply of these little cards in my glovebox, so that I can replace them quickly. Children can choose a card to take away with them to give to someone. Which message will they give to whom and why? By noting their choice of card and the person to whom they give it, you may get an insight into an aspect of their life that may be especially affirming or troubling, thus helping with your assesment of the child's world. One child chose a 'stop bullying' card to give to an older sibling, and after open-ended questioning, revealed abuse going on behind a foster carer's back.

On a final note, I always have a CD with me that appeals to most children. Walt Disney songs usually do the trick.

Just a little warning – having all these things in the car is, nine times out of ten, of great benefit. But be aware that they can make great missiles, so if you have a child in a tantrum on your hands, remove all the toys to the boot, preferably before you drive. If you don't know the child, start off with just one small soft item in the car until you find out if the child likes to throw things around as he travels – safety first at all times!

Most workers I have spoken to find their car is a very useful work environment. Unsurprising, when you consider all that it offers:

- Very limited necessity for eye contact, which many young people and adults we work with find difficult.

- There is a rhythm to driving that can be soothing.

- It is a safe space in terms of confidentiality. No one is going to knock and enter or just barge in.

- Depending on where you are heading, it can give a feeling of escape from daily life and all the pressures, if only for a short time. While getting to know a family I will sometimes take them to a park outside their area. It provides me with an assessment of how parents cope in a public space with potential dangers. It also gives the family a little break and I hope the parents may model my behaviour and bring the children back themselves on another day, thus improving the quality of life just a little.

- Lastly, your car is a bridging object between your personal and professional life. It tells people a little bit about you. You know so much about your families but they (rightly) know little or nothing about your personal life. Studies have shown that a little personal information shared can help build relationships. I remember when I was about nine years old I had an opportunity to go somewhere in the teacher's car. I remember she had a doll and a child's coat on the backseat and it was then I realised she was a mother as well as a teacher. That was a big revelation and I felt a lot less frightened of her from that point on.

Chapter 7

Common Misconceptions About Barriers to Working Creatively with Children

'I just don't have enough time'

This is the most common response I hear to working in this way with children. Social workers like me in practice teams are very pressed for time. Complex cases and lots of demands can contribute to a feeling that the worker is under siege, as indeed we often are. But working this way really does not take any longer than a home visit or taking a child out for a snack or drink of juice. It is productive in terms of good assessments, is child-centred and is a satisfying way to work.

When you first start, my advice is to choose three of the activities in this book that you feel would be particularly useful straight away. Alternatively, if you are feeling less confident, pick the activities that appeal to you, because if you like them, your enthusiasm will show when you present them to the child. To build your confidence, get together with colleagues. If each undertakes to prepare two of the activities (and to practise them), you will soon have built up a bank of activities, which will reduce individual preparation time. The child will keep some activities but the others should be kept in your desk or in the boot of your car, ready for use.

Spending 30–45 minutes with a child using a play activity is so valuable and it will give you more assessment opportunities than you may get from a straightforward home visit. This way of working will become second nature, in the same way as, for example, active listening. It is a fun way to work and, trust me, we really do have the time.

'My employer has no money to purchase resources'

The majority of the activities in this book can all be made for very little money, and once you have made them, they can be used again and again. If you consider how much it costs to take a child to a cafe, for example, most of the activities presented here cost less and will last for years.

'I am not very creative. I'm not sure I can make these activities'

Most activities can be made very easily. Ask older children to help with some of the resources for younger children, like *Mr Mad, Mr Sad and Mr Glad* (see pp.141–42). Most children could draw you fairly impressive angry, sad and happy monsters, and they will love the idea of helping you to help other children.

Internet search engines offer many images in pictorial or cartoon form that can be easily copied and printed off (but do check that there are no copyright restrictions). If you are like me – a computer illiterate – there is sure to be someone in the office who can show you how to find umpteen pictures, from elephants to fairies.

Photographs are another really good resource to use; you could also cut out images from magazines, which could be an activity in itself for an older child.

If you *really* struggle, or as a colleague said, 'for those who don't have a Blue Peter badge', why not ask an artistic colleague? In my experience, nursery nurses are very used to making resources, so perhaps you could tap into their skills. To help you, we have included a few templates for some of the activities in the appendices to this book (see pp.205–15), which can be photocopied.

'Can I do any harm working in this way?'

While these activities do direct children's play, you will not be putting them under any pressure because you will be listening and observing attentively and asking open-ended questions. Don't push a child to engage but rather offer the opportunity to do so. If it is not working, no matter how anxious or frustrated you feel, don't convey this to the child but simply offer a different activity or more free play, where you are directed by the child (see Chapter 3 on free play).

Focus on building your relationship with the child. Used in this way, these activities will never do any harm.

Chapter 8

Helping Us Talk Activities

Abused and neglected children are often very guarded. They have learned not to trust adults and have often been actively discouraged or even threatened against talking about what goes on at home. We need to keep focused on the children who are our clients, and in order to work effectively on their behalf, we have to take responsibility for enabling them to communicate with us. These activities have been created to help do this.

Henry the Heroin Lion
Purpose

- To give children the opportunity to think about the people around them, how they behave and how this has an impact on them.

What you need

- Good quality pens and paper (Option 1) OR

- pictures of animals in all shapes and forms (Option 2).

What to do
OPTION 1

1. Choose Option 1 if working with a child you know likes to draw. Begin with both of you free play drawing. Focus your own drawing on animals. Your pictures don't have to be good, just representational. The child will usually be interested in what you are drawing and ask you about them, so it is actually better if

your drawing is quite basic because you don't want the child to be put off drawing his own pictures.

2. Allow a little time for free play drawing and then encourage the child's natural curiosity to take an interest in your pictures. When the child asks about them, respond by talking about your picture and then say, 'Could you draw me an animal?' In this way you are moving from free play to directed play by asking the child to draw animals.

3. Give lots of encouragement and praise at this stage and then introduce talk about the qualities of animals, 'Oh, you have drawn an elephant. Elephants are very strong and they don't forget things.' Encourage the child to make his own suggestions.

4. After you have played like this for a short while you can say, 'If you were an animal which one would you be?' Follow this up with, 'That's good. Why would you want to be that animal?'

5. Next, ask what animals could represent mum, dad, gran, a teacher, a special friend and so on. You will have to judge how many, depending on how enthusiastic the child is.

This activity should generate lots of information and discussion about people close to the child and his behaviour that will help with assessments and therapeutic work (see the practice examples below).

OPTION 2

Option 2 uses photographs and pictures of animals you have collected and put in a box or folder (this is the easier way to do it!).

1. Look through the collection of photographs and talk about all the animals in the pictures and the qualities they have.

2. Ask which animal the child would choose to be and why. Do this with yourself and other people the child knows (as in Option 1). See the practice examples below as to how this activity develops.

Practice examples

Option 1

When working with a ten-year-old girl I had known for some months we were having an open discussion about her mother's heroin addiction. While we were engaged in free play drawing she expressed worries about her mother.

Audrey: 'I wonder if heroin was an animal, which animal would it be?'

Without hesitation she drew a lion and named him 'Henry the heroin lion'. I asked her to explain. She told me, 'He has big ears because he has to listen for dealers and big eyes 'cos he has to watch out for the police. He has big teeth 'cos once heroin bites you it has got you and big claws to hold onto you and not let you go. He is a lion 'cos I like drawing lions and they are very strong and heroin is very strong. My mum keeps taking it.'

I praised her for her drawing and noted how much she knew. We were able to continue talking about addiction and how it affected her mother and she agreed to show her mother her picture.

This in turn provided me with a way of visually demonstrating to the child's mother her child's views and understanding of heroin and addiction, and the fact that the child worried about her.

Option 2

I was working with a sibling group who had been actively discouraged from talking about their mother and problems at home. When I was working with them they were accommodated away from home and their mother was in a residential rehabilitation programme. The children were nine and 11 years respectively and both academically able. Neither was particularly interested in drawing, so after playing a board game they had a choice of games from my bag, and the box of animal pictures came out.

The younger child first chose pictures of two monkeys playing together to represent him, saying he chose them because he was good at being a friend, and then a picture of a dog wearing a hat, 'Because I am cute.'

The older child chose a picture of dolphins swimming together to represent him as he liked going swimming, and two kangaroos boxing as, 'I can fight if I have to.'

The younger then chose a picture of a sheep to represent his mother, "Cos she just does what her friends say, never mind us.'

His sibling chose a leopard draped across the branch of a tree, looking very sleepy, "Cos mum used to sleep all the time and we did all the work. I just thought that was normal.'

I asked if they could find any pictures of how they would like their mother to be. They chose a picture of a mother cat nurturing her kittens, 'See she is looking after her babies and giving them food,' and one of a dog running with a stick in its mouth, 'He's having fun and looks happy.'

Through this activity they were able to show me such a lot about life with their mother and were freed up to talk about what it was like being cared for by her when she was drug using. The boys were often angry but not able to talk about why. They possibly did not know why. Returning to use these pictures at a later session, we made a collage, naming and drawing the sheep and leopard's qualities. I then provided a picture of a lamb and a leopard cub. We stuck these onto the collage and wrote or drew how that baby animal was feeling about being cared for by a mother who only followed her friends and who slept a lot. We let lots of angry feelings out that day.

Right/Wrong Stones (Or: What to Do When the Child Remains Silent)

Purpose

Sometimes I meet young people who are unable to communicate easily with me. That doesn't mean that they are not engaged with me. They may feel that they have not elected to be there (for example, in the case of a forensic interview), but they have not walked out. They are observing me and usually listening even if they are not responding, trying to work out what I am about and what that means to them. In short, they are assessing me, the adult.

Most people who work with young people will have met this uncommunicative child. It is not an uncommon presentation, and is usually seen in children from 11 years onwards. From the child's perspective, it makes sense to be wary of a stranger, especially one who may be telling you things you do not want to hear or asking questions you do not want to answer. However, it can pose a real challenge to the helping adult, especially if you need to make a quick assessment of the child's safety.

The next stage of the child's presentation is usually to answer yes or no if asked a direct question. The third stage, in my experience, is when the young person answers more fully, but only in the context of the question you ask. For example, to the question, 'Can you tell me how things are at home?' the child keeps the answers to events strictly within the home, but may omit to tell you what is going on in a wider context. At this point the conversation is stilted, carefully controlled by the young person. Again this is understandable self-preservation behaviour.

The fourth and final stage is when the young person has developed trust and the conversation between helping adult and young person is free-flowing, open and relaxed. This stage is very rarely, if ever, reached in the context of duty appointments or forensic interviews; it simply takes time (probably months, possibly years) to get to this point with young people who have no reason to trust adults. To quote one of the young people I have worked with, 'D.T.N. is cool' (Don't Trust No one).

So what do you do when faced by a silent young person and you have to build rapport quickly and at least move them to the third stage in their communication with you? One of the tools I have used successfully is the *Right/Wrong Stones* activity, with a good dose of playfulness!

What you need

- A wide-necked jam jar. If you are concerned about safety, use a tin. This is not ideal as you can't see through it, but it will work.

- Lots of polished stones; you could use shells if you prefer, and I once used macaroni.

- Kitchen timer.

- Playfulness and voice intonation.

What to do

1. This is a very simple but fun game. Place all the stones on the table in front of the young person. Talk about the stones as you put them out, for example, 'I like this one best', 'Oh, look that one is an odd shape,' etc. You never know, this might actually get your child talking to you before you start, which has happened to me before.

2. Place the jar and kitchen timer between you both.

3. Explain the game:

   'We are going to take turns at seeing if we can get each other to fill the jar with stones. I will have a go first to show you how it's done. I am going to make a statement. If I get it right you put a stone in the jar for me and if I get it wrong you take a stone out. We will play for three minutes then count the stones and see how many I have. Then it's your turn to make statements about me and we will see how many you get. The person who gets the most stones in the jar is the winner – we might play the best of three.'

4. Explain the rules of the game:

   - No throwing.

   - Statements have to be made quickly and stones have to be moved in and out of the jar quickly (this keeps it moving and fun).

   - The person using the stones has to be honest.

   - If a statement is made that the stone giver doesn't want to answer, they can make a 'beep' sound and the statement maker has to make another statement. (You want to promote honest discussion but the child needs a get-out clause if he doesn't want to answer a question.)

5. Set the kitchen timer and off you go. You might make the following suggestions of statements:

   - Your name is…

- You are a boy/girl.
- We are in Lowergraton High school.
- You like chocolate.
- You live with…mum, dad, etc.
- You know my name.
- I am wearing a jumper.
- You are feeling scared.
- Adults can be pretty boring sometimes.
- You like school.
- You have a friend at school.
- I have got shoes on.
- You are wearing glasses.
- You understand why we are here.
- You are hungry.
- Computer games are cool.
- You don't need to go to the toilet.
- You don't like football.
- It's a sunny day.
- You have been hurt.
- You like macaroni cheese.
- I am wearing earrings.
- This room is too hot.

This list is not exhaustive, and you will need more.

TIPS

- Speak to someone who knows the young person before you begin. This person can give you some helpful ideas for statements that you can get right, for example which football team the child supports, favourite food, etc. Sometimes the young person gets such a surprise that you have guessed correctly that he forgets himself and starts a conversation. If that happens stop the game for a moment and go with it.

- Include lots of innocuous statements. This makes it safe.

- Don't be frightened to be a bit silly. If your young person is going to communicate with you there has to be something in it for him, and this could be having a laugh, getting your undivided attention or finding out about you.

- Statements about you that are not too personal really work. Young people are usually curious about the adults who work with them and learning something about you can give them a feeling of empowerment. Don't be afraid to use the 'beep' rule, however, when it is the child's turn to make statements for you to answer if questions get too personal or inappropriate. A mixture of statements about them, you, and the environment is best.

- If you are going to make a serious statement, for example, 'You have been hurt,' do it only after a considerable amount of time. This is when the best of three games comes in handy because you can make the serious statement the second time the young person is playing.

- Deliberately get some statements wrong and make some you are certain are right. These statements should be obviously right or wrong, for example, a statement like 'I am wearing a jumper.' This will help you check out that the young person has understood the game. Remember that people with dyslexia may find it hard to remember new instructions/sequences; children with a hearing impairment may not have heard all that has been said; and young people who are used to being talked *at* often don't listen well.

- Sometimes this game may not have the effect you hoped. The young person remains silent or monosyllabic. If that happens it's just the wrong tool for that young person (so maybe try another one), or the wrong day, or the wrong place. If you are in the child's home he may worry someone will come in. Family members as a general rule come and go as they please, and even if I have asked for privacy, the child's experience is that boundaries are not kept and people are unpredictable. Or maybe you are the wrong person for that child to feel safe with. This could be down to your gender or what a parent has said about you. Don't feel bad. If the best we do is no harm, then that's okay and this game played properly can do no harm.

- Even if no disclosure follows, it appeals to the senses and we know that attachment is built on sensory experience. Many of the children who access social work services have attachment disorders, so to help them make a connection with us, the use of sensory experience can be very powerful. Touch and sight are satisfied by the feel and attractive appearance of the stones. Sound is addressed in hearing the satisfying noise of the stones dropping into the jar (great for expressing frustration). Your facial expressions and voice intonation are essential for topping up the sensory experience, helping the young person to engage with you. The aim of the game is to build rapport in an unthreatening manner.

Practice example

In my experience the vast majority of young people will enjoy this game. There is usually laughter or at least a smile as I make silly statements or falter when they make an altogether too personal, rude or blunt statement for me to answer (I did warn you not to be shy about using the 'beep' rule yourself). But they usually get fed up with it after two or three games which is good and exactly what we want. It usually leads us into more easy conversation.

If not, try another tack. Could they suggest statements *they* think might be good to make the next time you play the game with a young person just like them? Responses might surprise you. Children have suggested I make statements about their safety and I respond along the lines of:

'Wow, that's a really important thing to find out because I could maybe help a young person in that situation. Could I ask you?'

This has led to disclosures of abuse. Children might be afraid of what will happen if they do tell, so to address this the conversation might go:

'You want to tell me about it but you're scared of what will happen.'

If the child confirms by plopping a stone in the jar, I would then give him information about what may happen, being honest:

'Can you tell me now?'

On most occasions this has been enough to release the child to speak. However, when this doesn't happen, try another activity such as *Safe Hands* (see pp.125–27) in order to leave the child with a suggestion of whom he may go to, to talk.

Traffic Lights

Purpose

This is a great activity to try when you really have to talk about something the child is reluctant to address (particularly if there are concerns about the child's safety and well-being). It still gives the child a degree of choice and control and offers the worker an assessment opportunity. It is also good fun to use and so should offer both child and worker a positive experience.

What you need

- A shoe box (or similar) covered in a black bin bag (or painted black) with three coloured circles stuck on vertically: red, amber and green to make a set of traffic lights. This will also act as your storage box for the activity.

- One toy car for each player.

- A4 paper cut into four strips (cut across the width of the paper – have lots and lots ready-prepared). You will use these to make cards with statements written on them (see below).

- Felt-tip pens.

- A kitchen timer (optional).

- Uncluttered floor space in a safe place. You need a level of privacy to afford confidentiality should the child talk about upsetting things. In good weather it can be played outside.

What to do

1. Come prepared with some of your cards written out already, with subjects you need to talk about, such as 'School', 'How you feel about living with nana', 'Mum's drugs'. Try not to have more than two or three serious cards. The rest should be fairly innocuous, such as, 'Your favourite flavour of ice cream'. You can write these at the start of the session, inviting the young person to give you ideas.

2. You also ask the child to write two or three serious cards. A young child I worked with asked me to write on her serious card, 'The sore tummy I get when I go to mum's'. After discussion and investigation we discovered her mother was feeding her out-of-date food.

   It is possible to use this with children who are not reading yet, but in that case you will need pictures of the topics. These could be photographs or pictures lifted from magazines or found using an internet search engine. In addition you need to check that the child understands how traffic lights work. Children aged four and above will usually be able to cope, but do check, as most of the children we work with have delayed or fragmented development.

3. Place the traffic lights at one end of the space, where they are easily seen.

4. Scatter the topic cards face up around the floor and call them parking spaces.

5. Explain the game. There are two ways I use this activity.

OPTION 1

'When I shout green, drive your car around the floor. (You will be holding your hands over the amber and red to indicate a green light.) When I say amber, get ready to stop. Think about which parking space you are going to choose and then when I say red you have to stop by parking in the chosen space. We will then have a chat about what's written on the card. Once we have used that parking space we take it away and I get to drive the car and you get to operate the traffic lights. The game is over when we have used up all the parking spaces. Then I think we will have juice as we will have worked hard. You might want to play with the cars and traffic lights in your own way while I get the juice ready.'

Give plenty of time for the child to drive the car around before you call the amber light. They should be allowed to have fun.

You may place some of the parking spaces under a table or in a corner. This makes them fun to get to and if the topic is difficult to talk about the child may find it easier if he can avoid direct eye contact with you while he talks.

If you have a sense the child does not want to talk about the subject (he may have persistently avoided that card or look uncomfortable) don't push it, no matter how important it is. Remember that the child has control over how much he shares with you. He will only tell you about difficult or upsetting things if he feels safe with you and trusts you. Pushing him into talking about something will only damage your relationship. It gives the messages you are not safe and that you don't respect/understand him. Instead, acknowledge his discomfort. Put the card away and then judge when it is the right time to see if he may be able to tell you why that subject was hard. You could say, 'We are not going to talk about…today but I wonder, can you help me understand why it's difficult to talk about this.' Or, 'I don't like to see you looking sad/upset. I didn't mean that to happen but I need your help to make me understand what the upsetting bit was.'

If you know you are going to have to talk about the difficult subject at some point, be honest. You might say, 'I know it's upsetting/difficult/scary to talk about…but we need to do that soon. It's important because (or we have to because)…but we won't do it just now. I am going to trust you to choose when we do it, either today or next session. Give me the card when the time is right. I know you will be brave and we will tackle it together.'

OPTION 2
Set the kitchen timer for about two minutes. Both you and the child drive the cars around the floor until the kitchen timer goes off. At that point you must drive into a space. The first person holds up the card and has to say or show, using the traffic light box, whether the topic is red, amber or green. A red topic is something the child doesn't want to talk about. Amber is something the child will talk about a bit and green is a topic the child loves talking about.

Take turns at talking about the subjects on the cards that you hold. Once done, set the kitchen timer again and off you go. The game ends when all the cards are finished.

Whose Job?
Purpose

- To provide an opportunity to discuss roles and responsibilities within a family, or indeed within any group of people (for example, a residential unit or a foster home). As an assessment tool, it creates an opportunity to find out who is responsible for what tasks or duties within the home and may reveal that children are bearing adult responsibilities inappropriately.

This activity is especially useful when children join a new home. It will give them the opportunity to explore differences and similarities and help them to understand their responsibilities in that household.

What you need

- Pens.
- Flipchart paper or a magic whiteboard.
- Reuseable adhesive (e.g. Blu-Tack).
- Quiet space – preferably with a wall you can stick flipchart paper onto (magic whiteboard sticks to almost any surface and leaves no marks when removed).

- Whose job? cards: these are simple, handmade cards (laminated if possible), with jobs or tasks written on them, such as:
  - washing the dishes/clothes; shopping for food; making breakfast; putting a brother or sister to bed; opening the mail, etc. (see Appendix III for a list you can photocopy).

What to do

There are several ways to use this activity. These are outlined below, but it is down to your judgement as to which will work best for your particular child.

OPTION 1

1. This is played one-to-one with the child. Explain that you would like to learn more about the child and how his family works and that every family is different and there are no right or wrong answers.

2. Ask the child to draw a picture of each family member using the whole flipchart sheet. This in itself may take a whole session, which is fine. You can chat about each person individually. Teenagers may prefer to write people's names. Encourage them to use the person's favourite colour or design the names in a way that tells you something about the person.

   One young man I worked with drew cannabis joints into the letters to tell me about his father, his comment being, 'He is always stoned, loves the weed.' Another very young child drew horns on his mother's head and stated, 'She is the devil.' Both children had a great deal to say about their home lives and this gave them the opportunity to begin to talk. When faced with such comments it is essential not to judge or show shock or surprise. Stay with the child and follow his lead. If his tone is conversational or matter of fact (in my experience this tends to be the case), your tone should be similar. Be a good listener – reflect back his statements. This lets him know you are listening and understanding. If you feel compelled to ask a question, ensure it is open-ended, 'Can you tell me more about that?' or, 'What happened then?' You may need to offer reassurance or positive affirmation, but most importantly, listen and ensure the child knows you are listening and valuing what he is saying.

3. Once the pictures are drawn to the child's satisfaction (not yours), stick the pictures on the wall. Remember not to rush it or try to get the child to put in lots of detail if he doesn't want to. Respect the child's wishes. If he stops and refuses to engage further, there will be a reason for this, so use another tool (maybe free play with the pens and paper) and revisit the activity another day.

4. You should now have a picture of everyone who lives in the household and any frequent visitors who play a significant role, for example, a granny who visits every week. Admire the pictures, notice who has been placed next to whom and perhaps gently explore the reasons behind this. 'You've put your dad next to your brother. Could you tell me about that?' Answers can range from comments around the relationships within the family to children simply stating the person was there because the space on the paper dictated where they went.

5. Next, lay all the cards face down on the floor and invite the child to pick one.

6. Read it with him and ask 'Whose job?'

7. Stick the card beside the person the child names. Have a 'Not sure' pile for the tasks the child cannot assign to anyone. If the child says, 'Nobody does that', ask if there is anybody *not* in the picture who does that to help the family.

    A young person (age 15) said nobody did that when he turned over the 'Keep things safe' card. When asked if there was anyone else who helped his family, he handed the card to me. This led us into a conversation about how he could help me to keep things safe. He conceded that he couldn't tell on anyone but that if we had a code word to alert me to problems, 'that would not really be telling.' At a later session, having been given the code word, I used the *Right/Wrong Stones* activity to check I was concerned about the right issue.

8. Continue turning the cards and expect some debate and hopefully some smiles.

9. At the end, reflect on the picture now in front of you.

    'Who has the most jobs?' 'How must it feel to be that person?'

    Ask if all the jobs are of equal value and which ones are most important to the child. Could the jobs be shared more evenly or are there some that just adults can do? Does anyone have a job that they shouldn't have? One 14-year-old boy stated that his mother dried and dressed him after his bath and he felt that that was his job now, not his mother's.

Which jobs are *not* being done? Do they need to be done? How can we make sure they are done? After this conversation it usually becomes clear to the child that we need the help of other family members to fix, or change, something. It is good practice to ask the child if he can think of ways to involve the family. If at all possible use the child's suggestion or at least part of it.

10. Make sure you keep a record, or better still, take a photograph when the child is satisfied with the placements. You may suggest either that you show the chart to the rest of the family or do it again with everyone joining in.

OPTION 2

This activity is done with the family, and will require:

- Whose job? cards

- a cloth bag with a drawstring top

- quiet space

- comfy seats

- ability to manage a family group and possible conflict (you may want to do this with a co-worker).

1. Gather the whole family together and explain that you are going to play a game with them that will help you to understand how their family works, but also give them the opportunity to really appreciate the things they do for the family and to praise each other. Explain clearly that there are no right or wrong answers as no two families are the same.

2. Place the cards in the bag. You hold the bag. This is important as it allows you to keep control of the game. You can ensure that there is no cheating, but more importantly, dictate the pace of the game and direct the focus back to yourself if conflict arises.

3. Ensure that the person choosing the card cannot read it before extracting it from the bag. To make it more fun, call out, 'Someone wearing red socks pick a card.'

4. Read the card aloud with the person. Don't assume that adults can read. Then invite the person to keep it if it's a job they do, or give it away to the person who does do that job. Again, have a 'Nobody does that' pile.

5. Carry on until all the cards are allocated, but be aware that it is possible you will encounter debate and almost certainly conflict at times. It's your job to keep things safe, so have a strategy before you begin about how you will manage the situation if it becomes heated. It will help if you know the family relatively well prior to undertaking this activity.

6. At the end, review the distribution of cards in the same way as in Option 1. Encourage family members to appreciate their own and others' contributions by inviting them to hold other job cards. How would it feel if they did that job? How would others feel about them having that job? Could they do it for a week to test it out? Then review it as a family group. If you do suggest this, it can be a positive way of effecting change, but you *must* support it with follow-up sessions if it is to work.

OTHER WAYS I HAVE USED THIS

When children are removed from their birth families and placed in the care of others it can be a frightening and confusing time. Perhaps one of the most unsettling aspects of this is the fact the child no longer knows what is expected of him. No matter how difficult his family experience has been he will have known his role and responsibilities within that setting. A little girl (age ten) I worked with knew that in her family it was her job to give her mother permission or not (as the case may be) to use heroin. It was also her job to keep her baby sister safe, as well as ensuring everyone was fed and looked after. Another young person (13) I worked with understood his role as the one who opened all the mail and ensured all the bills were paid.

Can you imagine how confusing it was for these children to be away from home? The girl was placed in a foster family, the boy in a residential care setting. Both, like every other child I have ever placed, were confused, overwhelmed and experienced a fear of getting it wrong. They found themselves in a completely alien environment. They wanted to be liked and to please their new carers, but how to do this if they didn't know how this new family worked?

Social workers and carers often worry about overloading a child with information and instructions when the child first arrives and this does need to be taken into account. But, given that one of a child's major anxieties will be to work out his role and to find the boundaries, it is worth addressing these areas quickly. I have done this exercise two hours after a child has moved and seen the child take a visible sigh of relief. Another teenage girl kept the Whose job? cards with her, folded into A4 paper with people's names on it, 'so as I remember and get it right, Audrey.'

I have asked myself if I increase the child's anxiety by doing this so early. Does the child then feel he mustn't get it wrong? I have now worked with many children and carers and conclude that for almost all children it reduces the anxiety. If they are unsure it gives them and their carers a common experience to refer back to. One carer reported the following conversation:

Carer: 'Remember we played the Whose Job? game with Audrey? Well this job is one we didn't cover. It's my job to paint the kitchen. Did you think it was yours?'

Child: 'Yes, my dad made me do everything.'

They decided that the Whose Job? game had frankly missed a lot of jobs out! They spent an evening making their own set which gave the child a way of telling the carer all about her family.

This tool can also be used to reflect on the child's changing understanding of roles. Compare the record of the first time you played it against six months into the placement. This can demonstrate where a child has relinquished adult responsibilities and which roles he has clung to. This will inform your assessment, but you can also use it as a means of helping the child to reflect on past experiences and perhaps the reasons he was accommodated (particularly in cases where the child has been neglected). I have also used it with a carer to demonstrate tangibly that progress has been made.

Whilst this tool has a serious purpose, *have fun with it!*

Spinning Wheels
Purpose

- To provide an opportunity to help a child make the link between choices he makes and the consequences of those choices. This can offer a way to clarify and increase the child's understanding of actions and consequences – both positive and negative – and to reinforce the message that the child is making a choice and therefore responsible for any consequence incurred.

It has been particularly effective with children and young people who are offending or engaging in antisocial behaviour.

What you need

- Two circles of card, approximately saucer size. With a pen, divide the card into about eight sections so it looks like a sliced pizza.

- Two arrows, about 1 inch wide, made out of card and attached to the centre of the circle with a paper fastener just firmly enough so they can move around, like the hands of a clock.

- Felt-pens.

What to do

1. Take one circle and write onto each segment a list of choices of actions the child might make and has made recently. Include those you would not endorse but which have been made by the child you are working with. Below are examples that a young person and I came up with:

Play football	Read
Make chocolate cookies	Steal a car
Speak to Audrey	Watch TV
Play computer games	Listen to music
Hang out with friends	Smoke

Phone mum	Go swimming
Use art room	Go for a drive with key worker
Play pool	Spend pocket money
Go to gym	Do homework
Use computer	Do washing
Visit nana	Help staff
Be disruptive	Count the pennies in your jar
Go skateboarding	Play board game

2. On the second circle write a list of consequences in the segments:

Feel good	Be popular
Feel satisfied	Get fit
Have fun	Lose trust
Feel proud of myself	Get in trouble
Feel content	Learn new stuff
Feel better	Produce work
Improve skills	Get praise
Get sick	Feel happy
Feel disappointed in myself	Have a better sleep
Be clean	

Introduce this with enthusiasm, emphasising that you have made it just for the child. He is then more likely to respond positively and he may take ownership of the spinning wheel, perhaps even showing it to others.

3. Begin by asking the child if he can find anything on the choices circle that he did yesterday. This should be easy, because your list will reflect his personal circumstances. Then talk about that in a conversational way and see if you can identify the consequence. It is important to emphasise that there is a consequence for every choice.

Sometimes children who are presenting challenging behaviour or regularly making poor choices think of consequences simply as a sanction for unacceptable behaviour without recognising the point at which a choice was made to follow that line of action. If they do associate consequences only with negative feelings, it can be hard to engage them in looking at how to change behaviour. They need to be helped to see that positive choices lead to positive consequences. It is very easy to understand how children only associate consequences with chastisement. Adults caring for children generally are very keen to help a child to attain acceptable behaviour. There is obviously good reason for this and it is reflected in society's expectations and views around behaviour. The focus then becomes around sanctioning undesirable behaviour and pointing out to children the negative consequences of their actions. It takes a skilled childcare worker to ensure that the child's positive choices are given as much or more attention and are referred to in a similar way (e.g. 'You chose to play nicely with your friends and as a consequence everyone is relaxed. Well done.'). It is common for adults to fail to comment on positive behaviour because this is what is expected of the child.

Children who have been neglected or abused and who have lacked basic nurturing care often fail to recognise or believe they can influence positive outcomes in their lives. Their experience is of negative outcomes and attention from those in charge of their care. These children are often operating at a younger developmental stage and many are stuck in the concrete thinking stage. If this is the case, a lopsided awareness of their ability to influence outcomes or consequences becomes debilitating. It can damage children's emotional health, self-esteem, self-efficacy and identity. Helping children to make the connection between action and consequence can be empowering and can build resilience.

Practice example

I worked with a child of seven, who sustained a serious injury. He came from a very neglectful home and on discharge from hospital was placed out of his mother's care and within a different community. He thrived in his new school and was described as 'settled', whereas he had presented extremely challenging, oppositional and aggressive behaviour in the school he attended when in his mother's care.

He was then returned to his mother's care and to the original school. The teaching staff were committed to this child and keen to have him return, but this was on condition his behaviour continued to be acceptable. However, he began to demonstrate the familiar negative behaviour (instigating fights, being cheeky to staff, etc.), so the staff immediately responded by implementing a behaviour modification programme. With a solid and united front they emphasised that actions had consequences. If he instigated a fight in the playground, then for a time-limited period he did not get to use the playground. At home his mother was also talking about consequences, 'If you had listened to me you wouldn't have got hurt and I wouldn't have a social worker. I hate social workers and it's because you didn't do as ye were telt that I am stuck with one. It's yer fault.'

After about two weeks of this going on, the little boy became withdrawn but not more compliant, refusing to work or follow instructions at school. He was sad and tired when I met with him and after using several other tools, I tried this activity with him. I focused on issues in school only, as I felt I had accurate reportage of what was happening. I had the choices and consequence circles ready and he could easily show me all the negative ones.

I then turned the arrow to, 'I listened to my teacher and tidied up the Lego when asked.' The consequence of this had been that the teacher had awarded him a few minutes more 'golden time' (free play at the end of the day). He could not easily identify the consequence of his good behaviour and needed considerable support to talk through what had happened. Furthermore, he found it difficult to think of other things he could do to elicit positive outcomes and lacked confidence in his ability to be good.

I initiated a programme of him trying one good behaviour choice each day. This required close communication between all involved. With his mother he would use his spinning wheel to choose a good behaviour, for example, 'Be kind'. His mother would alert the teacher unknown to the child, and the teacher would watch out for any example of this to praise it effusively. I was alerted at the end of each week and provided further positive reinforcement.

At later sessions we used the spinning wheel again and were eventually able to make new ones that were practically filled with positive actions and consequences.

The Tree

Purpose

- An assessment exercise particularly for older children of 14+ years and adults; it helps a discussion on resilience and stress.

What you need

- Pens.
- Paper.
- A quiet space.

What to do

1. Draw a simple outline of a tree with roots (you can enlarge the picture in Appendix IV). Talk about the tree, how the roots help draw water from the earth to keep the tree alive. The roots also grow deep into the ground to keep the tree fixed in high winds. The thicker, stronger roots help keep the tree rooted better than the thinner ones. Roots continue to grow throughout the tree's life and this adds to its well-being and safety.

2. Ask the person you are working with to think of himself as the tree in the picture and draw or write on the roots the things or people who keep him anchored and safe. Who looks after him physically and emotionally? What qualities does he have that keep him rooted?

3. Next, move to the trunk. This is the strong part of the tree. It moves very little, is solid to touch, easily seen, always there, keeping up the rest of the tree, and is the part that most other people have most contact with. Thinking of himself as the tree, ask the person to write on the trunk his strengths and the parts of him that the world sees.

4. Lastly we come to the branches and leaves. They are perhaps the most attractive and engaging part of the tree. They move in the wind, and the leaves change colour, hide other creatures in the branches, and when the seasons change, die off but grow again next year. Sometimes the branches get shaken about a bit when the wind blows. Ask the person to write down what would shake

his branches and what might affect the healthy growth of his leaves.

Note that I don't use emotive language, such as 'angry' or 'unsettled' or 'depressed'. I want to leave it open to the person's own interpretation. The roots represent the resilience factors in his life, the trunk any positives and strengths, and the leaves and branches vulnerabilities and stress factors. I don't used these terms until after the activity has been completed, when I explore with the person how to increase the resilience factors, strengths and positives and manage the stress factors and vulnerabilities.

5. To liven this up for adolescents who like making things, you could make a model of a tree with them out of a toilet roll tube, some card and crepe paper. Words can be written on stickers and placed appropriately on the tree.

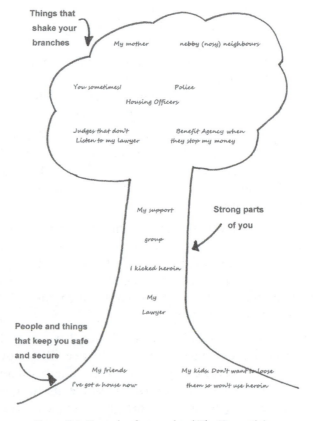

Figure 8.1: Example of a completed The Tree activity

Spider's Web
Purpose

- To break down the contents of an assessment report into manageable and understandable action points. It also identifies the person's own goals and any obstacles that might be in the way of achieving them.

I often come across clients who say they do not understand what it is I want them to do in order to get me out of their lives. The language we use in reports and in speech can be confusing and is often not clear enough. Or perhaps a parent has simply not connected their actions to the consequences. I have used this with young people of 14+ years, but mostly with adults. The visual impact of this activity helps engage people, but crucially the skill is in how you work it. Good humour, demonstrated by voice tone, facial expression and warmth, helps give the message that you accept the client, like working with him and you have faith in his ability to change. Combine this with a non-judgmental attitude and the ability to challenge in a firm, robust manner in a non-threatening way, and you have a powerful tool for change.

What you need

- Pens.
- Paper.
- A quiet space.
- The assessment report.

What to do

1. To prepare for the activity I go through the client's assessment report and highlight key concerns. I also ask the client to read through the report and highlight the words or phrases that have upset him or made him angry. More often than not we have the same points highlighted and this in itself can start discussion with acknowledgement that it can be a painful process. It might be that only the negative aspects of the client's life are being

brought to attention that is upsetting to him, or it may be that he cares and wants to do better.

Having done this, we should be at a place where the client feels listened to and less overwhelmed by the assessment report. In some cases he also begins to grasp that these are the concerns that brought about the allegations of neglect or emotional abuse and hence become more willing to engage with the process.

2. Begin by drawing a spider with long legs (there are templates for this activity in Appendices V–VII which you can enlarge). On the body of the spider write the main issue for the family/client that has been identified in the assessment report. For instance, this might be 'neglect' or 'physical abuse'. Along each of the spider's legs write an example that evidences the main problem. These might be:

- dog faeces in the home

- [child's name] saying he is hungry at school

- clean and dirty laundry mixed up together

- [child's name] dirty and smelly

Some spiders may end up with a few free legs; others may need many additional legs.

3. Using my face expressively, but keeping the tone gentle, I say something like, 'I don't like the spider much. What about you?' Invariably in response I get negative statements about the spider. Having established we don't like the spider, I continue:

> 'Well I've got good news for you. Birds eat spiders, so let me draw a bird for you. Now can we write on the bird what life would be like or how things would be different if it ate up the spider?'

4. Having drawn the bird, invite suggestions and write them on the bird. If the client is struggling, help him out. It may end up with statements something like this:

- The health visitor will stop nagging me.

- It will get rid of the social worker.

- It will get housing services off my back.

- I will feel better.

At this point I would not worry if all the statements were about getting rid of services and none were about the welfare, happiness or health of the child, parent or family. What we want to do at this stage is find motivation for change and start discussion.

'Now if only all birds could just eat the spider without any hassle or hard work. Wow! I would like a world like that. But the problem is spiders make webs around themselves (at this point I draw a web around the spider) so the bird can't get at them so easily. So, if we think of the web as being the things that stop us making changes or stop us having life how we want it (point to the bird), then can you write on the web the things that stop you changing?'

It is important to let the client lead here. He may find this part hard to do and may be resistant. This might be because admitting obstacles to change is about taking responsibility. But it could also be simply that he has not thought about it before and is trying to work it out and is struggling with the idea that he may be preventing change. So it is important not to dismiss ideas he comes up with.

For example, I may not think that money has any connection with dog faeces on the carpet, but the client is the expert on himself. If, in order to have 'street cred', your dog needs a special collar, then that may be the explanation for the dog faeces on the carpet – without the right collar, the dog doesn't get taken out, hence the faeces in the house.

When doing this exercise you may wish to gently prompt:

'So, if we look at this leg, "Amy is always hungry", we take that to mean she doesn't get enough to eat at home. Can you tell me why?'

Write the answer on the web, 'She doesn't like the food I give her 'part from crisps and sweets.'

Me: 'So maybe you need to stop giving her so many sweets and crisps and learn to cook some different things?'

Client: 'Aye well I buy those meals frae the [supermarket] – they're cheap.'

Me: 'Oh, so could we write money and food budget as the problem on the web?'

Client: 'Aye.'

You will note I was gently challenging the client, but negotiated for a reason we were both happy with. In order for this exercise to be productive, the client has to own it. It has to be the client's work. Problems and behaviour patterns have often been going on for years, sometimes generations, and all the issues are not going to be solved this way in one go, but it is a beginning and a small positive change is better than no change at all.

The real problem for the worker is when there are serious welfare or child protection issues which need to be owned by the client and addressed fairly quickly. With skilful questioning and negotiating, you should be able to reach an agreement on what to write on the web without compromising the issues. If not, then you have evidence for real concerns about the client's ability to change and to care safely for the child.

5. Once the web is filled and you are both satisfied there is no more to add, move on to the next step:

    'I feel rather sorry for that bird. It is a big web for him to clear up, so if we got a duster and cleared up the web he could get at the spider. Let's draw a duster and write on it the things that would help to clear the problems.'

They might look like:

- Help with food budget.

- Use the washing machine at the Child and Family Centre.

- Save up for a dog collar or ask aunt to lend me the money.

6. Once this part of the exercise is done, you can negotiate with the client the things you can help with and the things he needs to do, moving into task-centred practice (Lishman 1991). If there are a number of complex problems you may consider a family meeting or a bigger meeting with helping professionals. If you do this, help the client to share the exercise with them. It can increase confidence and provide motivation for change, and should be an empowering exercise.

TIPS

Before using this with a client, try it out first on yourself and then on amenable family and friends or colleagues. You will find that if you are honest with yourself and choose an issue that is real to you, it is not as easy at it looks to complete this activity, but it is worthwhile.

If the bird ate the spider and all the problems disappeared, what would life be like/feel like?

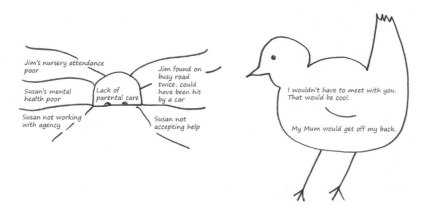

Figure 8.2: Examples of completed stage one of the Spider's Web

The problem is that the spider is inside the web and the bird can't get at it.

What is stopping you get at the spider – change your situation?

Figure 8.3: Example of comleted stage two of the Spider's Web

Who, or what, can help get at the spider? What will clear the web away?

(Client):   I am fine.   I don't need nothing cleared away.

I'm just doing this 'cause I like drawing.

(Social Worker):   Jim's not alright. I need you to get rid of the spider for him. We need to get rid of the cobweb. If we can't do it together, I will need to do it myself. I may need to take Jim into care.

(Client): I'll move in with my Mum. She will help with Jim.

Social worker suggests arriving at nursery ten minutes late and collect him ten minutes early to avoid the other Mums. Client agrees.

(Client): I won't see the Dr or nurse unless you go with me.

Social worker agrees.

Figure 8.4: Example of completed stage three of the Spider's Web

Onions

Purpose

- To get a young person or an adult talking about the different ways he presents himself to the world at different times, and the layers of his behaviour and/or emotions.

What you need

- Pens.

- Paper.

- Picture of an onion.

- An onion (optional).

What to do

Ideally I would create an opportunity to make onion soup as a warm-up exercise to this activity. As a busy social worker in a practice team I am unlikely to be able to do this, but in other roles (e.g. residential worker) I have been able to. I sometimes bring an onion in with me to cut in half so we can see the layers, but this is not always necessary.

1. To begin, draw an onion. Make sure it is big and shows the inside – all the different layers.

2. Point out to the young person that when we look at an onion from the outside all we see is its brown, shiny paper-like skin. This is like people. We all have an outside layer, a part we show to everyone. But if we cut the onion in half we see it has got lots of layers that can be peeled away. These are the parts we only show to some people or at some times. At the very centre is a small solid part. This is the very special part of us. Sometimes we show it but many people keep this part well hidden from the world.

3. At this stage reiterate the behaviour part of the activity:

   'People are a bit like that too. We have different layers to us. We have a way of behaving in school or at work or in the community and even at home.'

   And the feelings part:

   'We would be happy to tell almost anyone about some things about ourselves, for example what we like to eat, but there are other things we would only tell our best friend, for example our first kiss.'

   At this point check that the young person understands and is following by asking him to give you some more examples. This may happen spontaneously, before you have to ask.

4. Now decide whether to do a behaviour onion or a feelings onion (see below). With some young people your focus will be feelings, but this can be very sensitive, so I advise doing a behaviour onion first.

BEHAVIOUR ONION

1. To make a behaviour onion, ask the client to think of the behaviour he uses each day that he is happy for the world to see (the outside skin of the onion). This might include working hard, reading a book, playing with a dog, etc.

2. The next layer might be things that only school friends or people closer to him might see, like learning to speak French or changing his diet.

3. The layer under this might be what friends would know, and under that, behaviour known only to close friends and family.

4. Lastly, the central layers may include things that only he knows about his behaviour but is getting ready to explore with others. The very centre is his most private behaviour or thoughts around his behaviour. For example, this could include sexual behaviours or fears he has about his own behaviour.

   It is important to give the client permission not to write in any of these layers, but just to acknowledge that they are there – the aim is to provide opportunities to talk about behaviour, not to force self-disclosure. Sometimes just acknowledging that it is normal to have layers of behaviour is therapeutic in itself, and certainly some of the young people and adults I have worked with have been enabled to ask questions (sometimes couched hypothetically) about hidden behaviours they have been worried about. These have included ritual behaviour, some sexual behaviour, obsessive behaviour and behaviour around food. Mostly I have been able to reassure that these things are normal, particularly for adolescents, who have often been very relieved after our conversation. Occasionally I have advised that they may need further help and created the opening for them to get this.

FEELINGS ONION

1. The feelings onion works in the same way. Go through the layers with the client, talking about feelings. Often it happens that feelings and behaviour-talk crop up in the same onion, and if so, I just go with it. At the end I circle the feelings in one colour and the behaviour in another. It is helpful to separate this out as we can validate feelings and understand, but not necessarily condone, behaviour. Thus we can get to a place where we can acknowledge that sometimes feelings don't change but behaviour has to (for safety's sake or for it to become socially acceptable) if the person is to be accepted as a member of the community.

Practice example

I did a behaviour onion with a young person who was in a secure unit. Indeed, this activity was originally made for him. He was very much in control of his behaviour and often used it to manipulate situations. In my opinion he had developed this strategy as a survival mechanism and a lot of the time he was unaware that he was doing it. Some of the manipulation was very subtle. I needed a way to help him see the impact he was having on others and how much energy he was putting into portraying an image to the world. When I introduced this activity he did it enthusiastically and has allowed us to reproduce it here, as Figure 8.5.

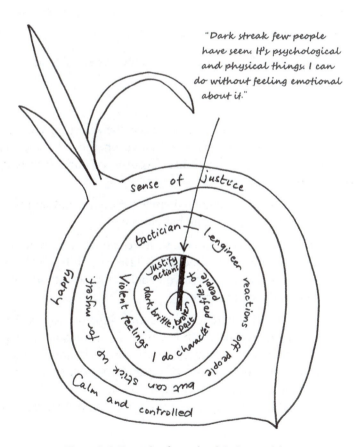

Figure 8.5: Example of completed Onions activity

Rainbow Talk

Purpose

- First and foremost, it is a relationship-building activity, but equally important, it is a good activity to begin an assessment with. It helps establish a child's favourite activities, foods, etc. It can also offer insight into the child's daily life and the resources available to the child.

What you need

- Good-quality felt-tip pens in rainbow colours.
- A3 paper or larger, with a circle of each colour from the rainbow drawn on it.
- Cloth drawstring bag (optional).
- A quiet, confidential space, preferably with a table in it.

What to do

1. Invite the child to choose a pen from the selection you have – each pen will match a coloured circle on the A3 paper. Have a chat about it. Is it the child's favourite colour? Why is it his favourite? And so on.

2. Explain that there is a coloured circle for each pen. Can the child find the circle for the pen he has chosen?

3. Using the pen he has chosen, ask if he can draw or write in the matching coloured circle one of his favourite things. (There is a list below of suggestions that you could write at the side of each circle before the child arrives.)

4. Repeat this with different colours and different topics. So, for example, if we assume rainbows have seven colours, that gives seven topics. It's good for adults to join in making their own circles as it provides a sense of equality. Also, if you know the 'Rainbow Song', sing it, as children love it.

    I make the following suggestions, but you can change these:

- Your favourite thing.

- Something that makes you happy.

- Your special toy/object.

- Your favourite band or football team.

- Something you think a lot about.

- Your dream house.

- The thing you like eating most.

5. Once all the drawings are done, put all the pens in the bag (or if you don't have a bag, you could hold them in your hand). Ask the child to close his eyes and then hold the bag out, and the child pulls a pen from the bag (or takes it out of your hand). Have a chat about the picture that was drawn in that colour of pen. Repeat this, taking turns, until you have discussed all the pictures. If you only have a very short time or you are working with a child with poor concentration, reduce the number of pens – you could use the other colours at another session.

Doll's House

Purpose

- To give children the opportunity to be in control of a family and/or a home.

- To give children the opportunity to talk about their home and perhaps to show you what happens in their home.

What you need
OPTION 1

- A straightforward doll's house with all the usual components such as furniture, dolls representing children and adults of different ages.

OPTION 2
You may decide you want a doll's house that is as similar as possible to the child's own home layout, which means making one with the child. This can stimulate talk specifically about the child's own home. Don't panic: this is achievable even for people who struggle with

handicrafts. It is really easy and only need be a representation, not an accurate model. The important thing is that the child sees it as his model of his home.

Let us assume the child lives in a high-rise flat/apartment block. To create this you will need:

- Three to four boxes of the same size. I use the boxes that contain photocopy paper at work, but cereal boxes, etc. work as well.

- Parcel tape.

- White or brown paper.

- PVA glue or a giant glue stick.

- Some coloured card.

- Broad felt tipped pens or paint.

- Furniture – choose pieces as similar to the furniture in the child's home as you can. Charity shops often have bits and pieces or you could make your own from small boxes and cardboard to make them look like the child's furniture. A bit of paint or a blanket or rug the colour of the item in the child's home usually does the trick.

- Doll figures – you could make pipe cleaner or peg people and this can be a great activity by itself. It invites children to create representations of the important people in their lives. You could do this as an activity prior to activity. I have found this always works well and is probably the ideal way to start the activity. However, if working with a child in the short term, you may not have enough sessions to be able to do this. In these circumstances I have a big bag of pre-bought doll's house figures of different ages, genders and ethnic groups. I also have a bag of scrap materials, scissors, thread, wool and glue so we can personalise the dolls to represent family and friends. I even have washable ink pens so a tattoo can be added if required.

What to do

To make the high-rise flat (this is just a suggestion to get you started, as it is important to remember that children love to make models and will usually have their own ideas. It is their home so let them do it their way):

1. Take one of the boxes and remove the top and one of the sides. Use card and tape to make dividing walls identical to the child's flat. You may want to paint the card so the walls are the right colour and add carpets to the floor.

2. Pile the boxes up with the child's flat in the appropriate place, that is, if it is a top flat, put it on the top.

3. Add a lift. The inner cardboard tube from toilet rolls, cut in half lengthwise and stuck to the side of the main structure, makes a great lift shaft. A smaller piece of tube, with a door cut out of it and a cardboard circle taped on the bottom for a floor, makes a great lift, with a piece of string tied to the top to enable the child to make the lift rise and fall. Lifts are very busy places and I have had a number of children play out scenarios from events in lifts.

4. Tape all three boxes together, adding the lift – admittedly often easier said than done. You will be glad of your child's help!

5. Cover this structure with the white or brown paper and invite the child to draw on the doors and windows and any other features the child suggests. Use this opportunity to explore who else lives in the block. This is a good assessment opportunity. Who does the child know? What experiences do they have of these people? Do any neighbours babysit for them? Do they have other family in the block? And so on.

   Now you have your block of flats. Remember to offer praise and positive comments for effort. Maybe take a photograph. Remember that you are not attempting a model building competition. As long as you have something the child is happy with and recognises as a representation of his home, you have done well.

6. Now, start working on the family and friends who live in the home. Be careful not to make limiting statements such as 'Let's find some dolls that look like your mum and brother and you.' By doing this you are assuming you know who lives in the house and missing an assessment opportunity. No matter how well you

think you know the family, *never* assume you know who lives there. People's circumstances often change quickly and things are often concealed from outsiders, particularly social workers. Instead I explain to the child that I would like us to find a doll for each of the people who live in, or visit, their house a lot. I tell the child that I know my dolls don't look much like the people he knows, but I have a bag of bits and pieces to help make them look more similar.

Before bringing out the dolls, make a list of all the people the child names as either living in or being a regular visitor to the house. I ask what feature makes them unique – 'Grandpa has glasses,' 'Mum's friend has black hair,' – and note this down if necessary. I then explain we may not be able to finish the dolls this session. This gives me a chance to find some black wool or make glasses out of wire. It is often useful to write out a list before bringing out the dolls because some children will want to use all the dolls and name people for each doll. In free play this is not a problem, but if you are using this as an assessment exercise, you want the child to think about naming the people actually in his home and not create a desire to use all the dolls and find names to fit.

The great majority of children, regardless of gender, love this activity. Self-esteem and self-efficacy are building blocks for resilience. Many of the children we work with have low self-esteem and poor self-efficacy skills. This activity allows the worker lots of opportunity for making affirming statements and giving praise, and, most importantly, the child has received undivided attention, been listened to and seen his ideas materialise.

It is also a good assessment opportunity in terms of finding out who the important people are in the child's life, who lives in the home and possibly who the child has contact with in his community. And it aids the assessment of the child's developmental stage in many of the important areas – motor skills, vocabulary and learning, ability to concentrate, to follow instructions and negotiate.

You could stop here and let the child take home his handiwork and enjoy it, but I tend to take it one step further, particularly if I have concerns but not enough evidence to take steps to protect the child.

HOW TO TAKE THIS ACTIVITY ONE STEP FURTHER

First, I negotiate with the child for me to keep the doll's house until our next meeting when we can have time to play with it properly. I usually suggest that I take photographs of the house for him while it is new and after the next session he can take it home with him. In my experience most children agree to this and in fact some don't want to take it home at all, fearing it will get spoiled at home. On the odd occasion, a child has wanted to take it there and then, and of course I agree to this, as it is his work.

Next time we meet, introductions to the session will depend on what I already know of the family. If I strongly suspect parental reaction to their child's work will be negative, I wait until we are alone to say in an excited tone, 'I've got a surprise in my bag for you.' Children who know me well can usually guess it is the photographs of the house. We can look at them and admire the model as we prepare to go into the session, and they will be given the option to take the photographs home with them. Should a child show them to the parent before the session and get a negative response, this could discourage the child from doing further work using the doll's house. Showing the photographs after the session at least gives forewarning of any likely negative response to taking the house back home.

Showing the photographs to the adult before the child takes the house home can give the parent time to prepare space for it. However, I have learned from experience that some adults will struggle to provide the response I am hoping for (that they will be delighted to give space to their child's wonderful creation). There may be many reasons for this: briefly, they range from simple lack of space to issues around the adult's belief that the child is being inappropriately rewarded or given importance. This may be an indicator for future parenting work.

At the end of the session discuss carefully with the child what he wants to do with his doll's house. Granny's home maybe a better place to keep it, or maybe it could stay at the social work centre for a bit longer or it could be taken to school to show the teacher. The child can still take the photographs home, but the model remains safe until the child decides what to do with it.

USING THE DOLL'S HOUSE IN FURTHER SESSIONS

Initially, I always let the child have free play with the house and dolls. This means that I don't direct or lead the play in any way. I remain child-centred and utilise aspects of person-centred counselling, for example showing I am interested by being emotionally and practically available for the child. I keep an open and interested expression and am alert to the child's direction or needs, 'Audrey, can you fix this?' Or 'Can you make him stand?'

I may ask the occasional open-ended question, 'Can you tell me more about what's happening there?' or make reflective statements, 'You are telling me that the mum-doll is playing with the PlayStation,' or 'You are moving the dad-doll outside.'

These reflections often lead the child to tell you more, just as adults respond to person-centred counselling techniques. But the primary purpose for me of these statements is to give the child the message, 'You are important. You have my attention. I am listening to you and available for you. I am with you in this and I am here for you.' I do believe that the children understand these messages. The evidence is in the trust that they place in us once a caring relationship is established.

Practice example

While using this activity with a ten-year-old girl I will call Mary, whom I had worked with for approximately six months, she acted out a number of scenarios before stopping her play and with disappointment said, 'Oh, I haven't got a "you" doll.' I reflected, 'You haven't got a doll that looks like me.' 'No,' said Mary, 'and I need one. I forgot to make you.' I responded enthusiastically, 'Don't worry. I have paper and pens in my bag.' She drew a picture of me and we stuck it with tape to a pen (note the importance of always carrying pens, paper, scissors and tape!).

Then she carried on and acted out a scene where the mother shouted at the children to clean and tidy the whole house. The mother hit out at the girl and didn't give her food if the home was not cleaned properly. The girl cried in bed. The next day the social worker doll arrived at the door. The mother doll answered it and Mary played out more or less exactly the visit I had done to the family two days earlier. This included me walking round the flat holding Mary's hand and my compliments to the mother on the effort she had put into tidying the home.

Just prior to this visit I had been contemplating the need to accommodate Mary as there were serious issues of neglect.

Watching the scenario play out before me I had a lot of clarification questions forming in my head, but I knew it was important to allow Mary to finish her story.

Mary proceeded to make the social work doll leave the home. With the doll figures, Mary acted out the children eating, and the mother smoking and not answering the children's questions and then going to sleep.

Having played this out Mary sat back on her heels and said, 'There. That's our house for you. I've told you now.' She then began to cry. I comforted her and told her how brave she had been. I clarified that she had shown me a real scene from her home and not made up a story. I thanked her for showing me what happened at home. Note, I didn't say *telling me*. Children are very often given strong messages about not telling. I said that I was sorry if my visits had made life harder for her. To this she replied, 'She hit us anyway and we never got chippies then so it was better and I like you visiting. I don't mind the cleaning up much.'

I told her I thought she was a brave girl and that I was going to have to ask a nice police officer I knew to help me get things sorted out and that I would need her to tell us her 'how things were at home' story again. Mary just shrugged and said that was okay.

After ensuring that Mary had a good lunch and time to play in the park to release some of the nervous tension, I conducted a joint interview with a police officer. During this interview Mary explained the same set of circumstances without the use of the doll's house but held the dolls in her hand. She also described other incidences of abuse and acts of neglect and accurately described her mother's use of heroin. Her younger sister (aged four) was also able to describe life at home through the use of the play area at the child and family centre. This matched her sister's account. I was able to secure a child protection order on the basis of their disclosures, as the mother would not agree to voluntary accommodation.

The children were placed with a relative and subsequently that relative has provided them with a permanent home. In the following weeks Mary and I made a model of her new home and she was able to play out happier scenes.

REFLECTIONS ON THE USE OF THIS ACTIVITY

In Mary's session there was no need for me to instigate discussion around family life and routines as it happened naturally, and this is usually the case. But when children have been deprived of play opportunities in their early years, or have some developmental delay, it can be useful to guide them a little. I will only do this after I have allowed the opportunity for free play and the child is now disengaged or has not initiated any play. In this case I might say to the child, 'Can you show me where all the furniture goes in your house?' and then I may ask, 'Can you show me what happens in your house in the morning (or at teatime, bedtime etc.)?'

As soon as the child becomes absorbed I revert back to child-centred interaction, employing some of the person-centred counselling skills as mentioned earlier. It is noteworthy that older boys sometimes appreciate being given a question that leads or directs their play. I suspect this may be around gender stereotypes as to who plays with doll's houses. Being given a task, 'Can you show me...' allows the boys to play with the doll's house. The construction of the doll's house can stimulate older boys into talking about events in the home. Some who are resistant to making a model house will agree to make it ostensibly for a younger member of the family. In my experience, once started, the majority of boys relax into the play and get a great deal out of this activity.

Cartooning
Purpose

- There are many different purposes for cartooning, but the overriding one is to support communication using a medium that is familiar and fun and acceptable to any age range. Cartooning can help a child to describe an event in a clear and sequential manner (which is particularly useful in child protection work). It can be extended to:

  o look at how situations could have been changed by different actions

  o help develop self-awareness of the process of thinking, feeling and doing, and can also help to develop empathy

○ help children develop an understanding of social norms, becoming a social story that a child can refer back to for guidance.

What you need

- Good-quality felt-tip pens.
- Large piece of paper, at least A2 size.
- Table to work on.
- A quiet and private space.

It is very important to have good-quality materials that are presented well. It conveys the message that you respect the child and place a value on what you are doing with him. Large paper is important for a number of reasons. You need to make your cartooning boxes fairly large, as young children's motor skills are not as refined as an adult's and they simply need more space. Asking them to work on small paper is challenging for them and requires concentration – the focus of concentration should be on the cartooning, not on how to fit the picture onto the paper. It is not uncommon for the children we work with to have developmental delay, so some older children/teenagers may benefit from the larger paper too. It is perfectly possible not to know of any developmental issues prior to working with them, especially if you have not met them before, so my rule is 'big bits of paper won't go wrong.' (Don't worry about storage later or attaching it to a report because you can always use a photocopier to reduce it to A4.)

If I am planning to do this cartooning activity, I will already have the paper marked out before the session (see the example in Appendix IX). (Note that I use 'thought' bubbles and under each box a space for 'feelings'. This allows the child to consider what he felt, what he thought, what he did and what was said.) But the beauty of this tool is that you should be able to use it at a moment's notice. I have used it when investigating a child protection concern. To date, I have not used it in a forensic interview, but potentially you could. It would then need to be submitted as evidence, however, so the police officer would need to take it away as a production for court. In this case you should explain to the child what is going to happen before you begin and offer a photocopy for him to keep. Most children can accept this.

Remember that a child who gives you his artwork is offering you a precious gift, a part of himself, and we shouldn't assume that he will be happy to give it to us. Social rules dictate we don't normally ask for gifts in such a direct manner, so think it through and respect the child's wishes. If he doesn't want to part with his drawing you shouldn't take it, but you will need a plan B in terms of how to deal with your need to have a record of it. Ask for permission to make a photocopy. You are there to listen to the child and this may lead into a decision to allow you to take it. Just demonstrating that you listen and care about his views helps build a sense of trust.

What to do
There are many ways to begin and to some extent it will depend on the context when using this activity.

USING IT SPONTANEOUSLY
I have often been in situations when children are upset and trying to tell me lots at once. They are in a hurry to get it all out or maybe so much happened it is all jumbled up in their head. I need to slow them down and help them to sequence what has happened, and hopefully give detail.

USING CARTOONING IN A PLANNED WAY
I tend to use cartooning in a planned way when I have a specific problem to tackle. The only difference in the preparation is that I prepare the paper into a cartoon strip and sometimes add feelings boxes. The thinking part comes quite naturally by adding thinking bubbles as you go, as well as speech bubbles.

The child will be aware prior to our session what we are going to do, as we will have agreed it previously. The idea of using cartooning may have come out of a discussion, for example, about bullying, where the child is either the perpetrator or victim, or it may be about non-school attendance, or perhaps about mealtimes, when everyone gets upset and angry. The possibilities are endless, but in planned work cartooning is always used to tackle a specific issue or problem.

Practice example

On visiting a child in school for a routine session, she appeared upset. I invited her to choose an activity from my bag but she was not interested. As I had known her for a while and established a relationship, I asked what was wrong. She described how her father had asked her (the child's) permission to leave her unattended. After her father left, the little girl had got scared and decided to go to her aunty's house which was close by. On the way she was stopped by the police who were obviously concerned to see a little child out on the streets alone. She was upset while telling me this.

I listened very carefully to everything the little girl said. She was very upset and crying. Because I knew her well and knew she appreciated physical comfort I held her hand in mine at points and at other times gently pushed her hair away from her face. I used all the skills you would utilise in person-centred counselling (Rogers 2003). She was speaking quickly but I worked hard to ensure that at some points I made reflective statements.

Once she had finished I was left with a sense of what had happened but no real clarity about the event, which I needed, and also at this point I did not know she thought the police had been angry with *her*, although her distress was clear.

I thanked her for telling me. I commented that everything she had said was very important and I thought it must have been scary and upsetting. At this she nodded furiously.

I commented that she had had a busy time (the child nodded and cried). I explained that I wanted to make sure I understood properly because she was important to me, and I wanted to make sure I helped in the right way. I stated that it was a bit like going to the doctor with a sore bit. He needed to find out the symptoms before he knew which medicine to give, didn't he? (The child nodded.) Could she help me to make sure I had understood properly? The child said yes.

'Okay, I've got a cool idea. Why don't we make a cartoon strip about what happened so I can see the pictures and read the speech bubbles too. That would really help.'

The little girl was more than enthusiastic. She jumped up to go and get a big piece of paper. On her return she was more composed, and very focused (both children and adults alike can find comfort in being proactive in doing something to alleviate distress).

I folded the paper into squares to mark out boxes for the cartoon. She needed help to work out where to start. I suggested, 'Why don't you start when dad was still with you?' I could have suggested she start when her father asked her permission to leave, but I very deliberately didn't. I left the time frame fairly open because at that point I had no idea what had happened beforehand, and I wanted the child to have the opportunity to include anything prior to the point of her father asking to leave, which she may have forgotten about when telling me earlier.

The next part of the process simply involved me utilising attentive listening skills and offering reflective statements and empathy as and when required. In addition, I would occasionally ask an open-ended question. This stimulated more discussion or sometimes additional detail being added to the cartoon. On completion of the cartoon I admired it and commented on its contents. This allowed me the opportunity to give the little girl lots of positive feedback, 'You were so brave to go and find aunty.'

I also used this opportunity to discuss other people's actions, thoughts and feelings. This allowed me to explore the child's perspective further but it also gave the possibility of work around empathy. 'I wonder why daddy went out?' (This was said in a soft voice almost to myself, to give the child the option as to whether she answered or not.) I also ignored the explanation in the cartoon that her father wanted a cigarette, as I was 90 per cent certain that was not the case. The child replied 'I think my daddy's doing stealing again with the man with the red car.'

I explored with her the interaction with the police officer. 'Now the police man said, 'How old are you? Where are you going?' What do you think he was thinking?'

Child: 'She is a bad girl for being out late. I am going to arrest her and put her in the cells.'

Audrey: 'Oh! Okay, so what do you think the policeman was feeling?'

Child: 'He was feeling angry.'

Audrey: 'Hmm, you think he was angry?'

Child: 'Yes he was.'

Audrey: 'Oh, who with?'

Child: 'Me.'

Audrey: 'Wow! I hadn't thought about that. Hmm, want to hear what I thought the policeman might have been thinking and feeling?'

Child: 'Go on then.'

Audrey: 'Well I thought the policeman would be thinking, 'Oh dear oh dear there is a brave little girl out so late. I wonder how old she is? I wonder if I can help her. I wonder where she is going. I will need to find out quickly before my radio goes and I need to go somewhere else. I feel really worried about her and I am a bit cross with mum or dad. They should be looking after her.' What do you think? Could the policeman have sounded grumpy 'cos he was worried about you and cross with your dad and in a hurry?'

Child: 'Yeah, maybe.'

Audrey: 'You know you did all the right things. You are a good, brave girl.'

Child nods.

I was careful not to dismiss her ideas of what the policeman was thinking and feeling. Sadly, most of the children I work with (and certainly this little girl) do not have positive experiences of adults in their lives. Her life experience has taught her independence and a mistrust of adults, so presenting her with a different possibility and helping her to question her own interpretation, was far more effective.

As a follow-up I found out who the police officer was. He agreed to meet the child with me and tell her that he had thought she was brave and sensible and that he had been grumpy but this was with her father. He apologised for scaring her and assured her she had done the right thing.

This little girl now 'quite likes' police officers. Previously she had been afraid of them and disrespectful. The follow-up reinforced her learning in a way that was physically tangible. Again and again, I have found that multisensory learning is most effective, especially when working with children who have attachment disorders.

1. The first part of the process is the same as described above. However, now you are looking to solve a problem, so you want to create different possible endings. To do this, create the initial cartoon strip of the incident. Then, provide the child with a new, blank cartoon strip. Place this over the original strip at the point you want to change it. For example, if in Box 5 the child has portrayed a friend asking them to steal a sweetie, and then in Box 6 they do steal the sweetie, lay your blank strip on top of Box 6 and ask the question, 'What could we draw that would be different?'

2. Follow those actions to a conclusion and compare with the original strip. Set a challenge as to how many different cartoon strips the child can create. He could ask other children, teachers, parents, carers, the shopkeeper (but go with them and warn and prepare the shopkeeper first). By doing this you are effectively looking at antecedent behaviour and consequences with the child. In addition, you are asking what the people in the cartoon were thinking and feeling, so potentially empathy work is going on. Remember to do this for all the characters in the cartoon.

Don't get too serious. I did a lovely piece of work with a child about stealing and lying and the main characters in our cartoon were Ben 10 and Scooby-Doo! Scooby turned out to have very high morals indeed and Ben 10, I discovered, was a bit of a chancer. The use of the cartoon character emerged because the little boy I was working with was not interested in cartooning people. He was oppositional and resistant to addressing any of his behaviours and did not want to meet his new worker. He knew all about workers. He told me that he wasn't going to work with me because I had 'come to work with him to stop him telling lies and stealing'. I replied, 'True, but you know what I am good at – drawing Scooby-Doo? Come on let's get my paints out and you can give me marks out of 10.' (I had spotted that he was wearing a Scooby-Doo t-shirt and was hoping he was a big fan.)

I had this conversation in the car park of a residential school. I arrived as the child was trying to run away from a residential worker and I simply stepped in his path. I knew that if I didn't hook this child into working with me instantly, it would take weeks to even establish a rapport. Having blocked his exit and noting the residential worker had caught up and was on hand to help if necessary, I sat on the ground and started to pull out the paints from my bag. He looked surprised and stood watching. 'You're crazy. Can't paint here. You got to paint in the art room.'

'Aw, but I want to paint Scooby-Doo here right now!'

I knew this boy could relate to that right-now feeling because he had been labelled as having conduct disorders, and for him that meant as soon as a thought popped into his head he had to act on it. As I persisted in mimicking something near his own behaviour, he became very mature and responsible and insisted we go to the art room to paint.

The purpose of my behaviour was:

- to engage him quickly

- to convey we may have something in common, that is, Scooby-Doo

- to act on the possibility that he might get the message that I understood the behaviour that he often displayed and which regularly got him in trouble.

After establishing a boundary by blocking his exit and demonstrating that his residential worker and I were communicating effectively with each other, I quickly put the child in charge, moving to child-centred practice within safe limits. So I allowed him to take me to the art room. We painted Scooby-Doo and he gave me some frank feedback on my work.

That's all we did that day, but the next time I had prepared a cartoon about what had happened and together we used blank strips to work out other possible outcomes. From this point on we used cartooning on a regular basis. Sometimes I asked the staff to draw a cartoon of incidents that had happened from their perspective. We were then able to compare the child's cartoon of the same situation with the staff's. It became a good mode of communication and a catalyst for change.

USING CARTOONING TO SUPPORT CHILDREN'S SOCIAL SKILLS

Some children, for a variety of reasons, don't pick up social cues or may find it difficult to transfer social learning from one situation to another. Sometimes cartooning can help in these circumstances. You could make a cartoon strip that depicts what will happen and what the expected response is. For example, you might make a cartoon strip about going to the doctor (routine situations are the best to start with):

- Box 1: Getting ready – having a wash, putting on clothes etc.

- Box 2: Travelling to the doctor's.

- Box 3: Telling the receptionist you have arrived.

- Box 4: In the waiting room.

- Box 5: Being examined by the doctor.

- Box 6: Returning home.

This allows you to talk through what is likely to happen. Leave the speech bubbles blank and fill them in with the child as you talk about it. I might just do simple linear drawings so the child could colour each picture in as we talked. However, bear in mind some children might see colouring in as 'work' and prefer to have the completed picture before them as you talk.

The child could then take this cartoon away and refer to it as often as he wished. This should provide reassurance and reduce anxiety and might help him to respond appropriately. Some may need to be reminded to look at their cartoon as a prompt for them to know what to expect and what is expected of them.

Figure 8.6: Cartooning to support social skills

Scales and Scaling

Purpose

- Many who read this will be familiar with the concept of scaling, which is used in solution-focused therapy. I have adapted it to use in my work with children and families. My primary aim is to try and identify issues affecting the family or the child and to get some measure of the impact or value for the child/family. Scaling can be very effective in creating the opportunity for change. It can be a good starting point when beginning to work with a child or family, and it is useful for reviewing situations.

- Thinking about what needs to change for the child to move up the scale towards the positive goal encourages finding solutions within the family rather than having them imposed on them. It also gives me a way of measuring if the person feels the same way about the issue consistently, or whether the impact and value goes up and down. Is there a pattern to this? Has this been influenced by a change within the living environment or school, etc.? Or maybe even by my intervention?

- When used in a family group it can reveal useful and sometimes surprising information about a family member's thoughts or feelings, challenging assumptions and habitual roles that have been prescribed to individual members in the group.

What you need

- Scaling strip: get a piece of card about ten inches long and two inches deep. If you have time, colour it in, changing the colour for every 1-inch. It is most effective if you can grade the colours from hot (red, orange, yellow) to cold (shades of blue and green). The colours should blend into each other. Then write the numbers 0–10 along the length of the strip. Lastly draw a little character on another piece of card (I favour a teddy or a spaceman) about three inches high and cut a hole in their tummy and make vertical slits on each side of the card. These slits should be long enough to enable the character to be threaded onto the strip. The hole in the tummy allows the number on the scale to show through. You should then be able to slide the character up and down the scaling strip. You will need more than one if you are working with a family, so keep a template. It can be tricky to get the character correctly fitted onto the scaling strip, but don't give up. The children and parents love them.

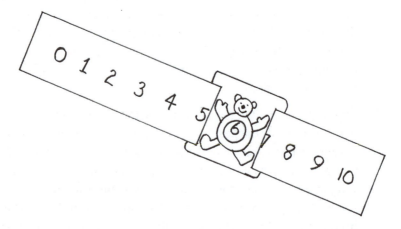

Figure 8.7: Scaling strip

What to do

1. Explain that sometimes it is hard to say how much you like or dislike something, and this is a way to measure how you feel. It is important to explain clearly that you scale 'in the moment', based on what you think/feel right now.

2. Begin to play with the scale.

   'Can you show me how much you like chocolate? If zero means you hate it and don't like it at all, and number 10 means you love chocolate, it's your favourite sweet, show me where you are on the scale.'

   'Wow! You really like chocolate. It's away up at number nine. What would make chocolate go to number ten?'

   One little girl said it would go to ten if it was Smarties as they were her all-time favourite.

3. Continue to practice with subjects that are fairly innocuous as this helps the person get familiar with the scale. Maybe he could ask *you* a scaling question? If he agrees to do this, model how to use it by speaking out loud the thought process you are going through to decide where on the scale you are.

4. Use your judgement to sense when people are getting comfortable scaling and answering questions related to their scale. When you feel ready, move onto more focused scaling questions. For instance, you could use scaling to help a child who is accommodated away from home tell you how contact with the birth family is going.

   'I know it's quite hard to talk about it (gentle, reassuring voice) but this way you could get teddy to help you show me. Hey! Let's give it a go. (Said with enthusiasm). If zero means you don't like having orange juice at contact and ten means you love to drink orange juice at contact, get teddy to show me how you feel.'

It is very important to start with a less emotive subject and to break each aspect of contact down and to scale it. Going in too directly, 'Zero is you hate contact with mum and ten is you really like contact with mum,' would risk an inaccurate picture of the child views, as it is too wide. They may scale to indicate they hate contact, but what they actually mean is they hate contact time being too short.

Remember that young children think in a very concrete manner, while adolescents frequently answer only what is asked directly and then often in one word. This means that the language you use is very important. Direct, clear language works best.

BIG SCALES

When working with children, adding an element of fun and play is, I think, almost always essential. It keeps the children interested, rewards everyone involved emotionally and provides a good model to parents/carers. A child's work is their play.

Big scales are great for working with very active children and for work with family groups.

What you need

- Ten paper plates.

- Ten different kinds of textured/coloured paper, card, material.

- Glue.

- Self-adhesive covering film (purchased from stationery shops).

It's good to get the children to help you make these big scales. Draw big numbers from 0–10 on the coloured paper, cut them out and stick one number on each plate. If you want to be able to use the plates over again, cover your numbered plates in the self-adhesive film. Now you have big scales.

What to do

1. Place the plates in numerical order in a row on the floor. Explain what scaling is, as above. But this time invite people to go to the numbered plate, pick it up and hold it above their head. Alternatively, when working with an individual child who is very active, asking him to sit down on top of the plate can help – sitting down usually results in calmer behaviour than standing up.

2. Start with subjects that are easy (likes and dislikes) and common to all the group members. When working with a family group at this stage you are observing alliances, possible domination by a family member(s) and family responses. In sibling groups it is not uncommon to find the younger children looks up to the older

ones and wants to follow them. It is also healthy and common for children to model their responses on their parents, but this is different from an observation which suggests that there is a fear of deviating because to do so risks an undesirable consequence. Is there any watchfulness present or a sense of anxiety? If you observe this, you will need to make a decision as to whether to proceed or end the game after trying out the initial innocuous scaling questions. In this case, follow this exercise with another activity – the family will not be aware that it has been cut short.

Depending on the family's circumstances and taking into account your role whilst also giving careful consideration to the children's safety in the broadest sense, you may choose to use your observations at a later date to challenge a person's behaviour. This can be very a powerful tool, which is why you have to consider carefully whether to use it or not.

If you decide to proceed, then have fun. Think about who you are going to ask to go first or whether you should ask everyone to stand up and go to their numbers at once. This may simply depend on space and noise level. Once everyone is standing, holding their plate, begin the questioning phase. If more than one person chooses the same plate they can either all hold the plate or leave it on the ground and stand around it.

In my experience group participants are usually very interested in each other's reasons for their point on the scale and this should be encouraged. But it is important that you keep control and make sure no one feels ostracised for their reasons. If you are worried about this, just stay with the innocuous questions, and don't underestimate how invaluable this can be.

AN OPTIONAL ENDING ACTIVITY

As an ending for this activity, I often provide stickers and a small lucky dip bag containing compliment cards, a small chocolate and so on, and invite family members to give each other these, plus the promise of one nice thing that can be done when I am not there. Maybe this could be to give someone a smile, sing a song, draw a picture, give a hug or tell someone something you like about them. This ending exercise in itself can be very powerful and can take a lot of time when people are not used to doing it. Give this exercise the time it needs because if the family grasps it, enjoys it and uses it, you will have given them a tool that could change their lives.

Practice example

I was working with a family where the father had seriously assaulted the five-year-old child. We did scaling as a family group and I used innocuous questions. I asked, 'How much do you like ice cream? Zero means you really, really don't like it, and ten means you really, really like it lots.' The mother and father scored nine and ten respectively, but the five- and seven-year-olds went to zero. This brought protest from the mother who stated that they liked ice cream. I said we needed to listen to what the girls were telling us and if they scored at zero then that was okay. I invited the mother and father to sit down then I praised the girls and asked a series of other questions around ice cream for them to scale. 'How much do you like the taste of ice cream?' They both scored ten, which indicated that the ice cream was not the issue. They clearly liked to eat ice cream, so it had to be an issue with the circumstances around eating it. I was aware the family did not own a freezer and that an ice cream van went round the housing scheme, so I asked a series of scaling questions around when the van arrived. From these questions it became clear that they did not like the music that announced the van's arrival. I was still puzzled and so asked the oldest child to ask the younger sibling a scaling question to show me what the problem was. She asked, 'Show how much you hate it when dad gets angry 'cause he can't find the money for the van and he wants us all to eat ice cream. Zero is you're scared.' Both girls stood on zero and their mum went to join them. I looked at the father. He had his head in his hands crying. He spontaneously said sorry to his partner and children and asked to go to anger management, something he had previously vehemently resisted. I finished by helping family members to reflect on how much we had learned together about each other.

Beads and Badges

Purpose

- To remind a child how many people they know and are connected to.

What you need

- A large selection of different, colourful beads – you can buy old necklaces from second-hand/charity shops and split them up.

- Thread – elastic thread is good for children, but check the beads fit as it is thicker than normal thread. Embroidery thread can be used but doesn't have the same stretch value.

- A quiet, confidential space.

What to do

This is a very simple activity but it has proved to be very effective.

1. Show the child all the beads. Start by picking some out, describing and admiring them. Ask the child if they would like to make a bracelet. I've never had a refusal yet, but if a child does refuse, suggest you make a chain of beads, and if still not interested, change the activity.

2. Presuming the child says yes, explain that they are special beads, so there is a little rule attached. He can have as many beads as he wishes *but* he has to name a person who knows him for each bead. For example:

   'That little bead there is brown with gold stripes and you know I have a stripy cat, so you might choose that bead to use on your bracelet and help you to remember that I care about you. Now, can you choose a bead for…hmmm…your teacher?'

Carry on with this, helping the child to think about all the people in his life. With relevant people, try and name a quality suggested by the relationship, 'You've chosen this bead for your teacher and I know she loves it when you dance and has said you are good at helping.'

Include people such as the local shopkeeper, 'lollipop' lady, etc., especially if the child has only a limited number of people around him.

3. Once you have made the bracelet (or maybe it has turned into a necklace because you have so many beads), make a real fuss when the child puts it on. Emphasise its importance, how beautiful it is, how well he has made it and how many people know him. Think about who would like to see it. Could the child show it to some of the people who have a bead on the bracelet?

A word of caution: these bracelets/necklaces do get broken and lost so try to keep some identical beads safe so that you can make a replacement if necessary. You may also wish to jot down the people the child has named. It will potentially give you an idea of his support network. You may be able to utilise this knowledge in developing his care plan.

AN ALTERNATIVE, IF BEADS DO NOT APPEAL TO THE CHILD
I choose to use beads as they are easily portable and the child can keep them on his person. They also meet two of the five senses – vision and touch. We know vulnerable children often lack sensory care, which is so critical to early brain development. However, beads may not appeal to all children. Some may view it as 'girls' stuff' and others not find your selection aesthetically pleasing.

In this case you could use badges. They can be picked up in charity shops or get friends and colleagues to collect/donate for you. You will need a selection with interesting logos on them, for instance a tiger's head that could be for brother Jack who likes the story, *The Tiger Who Came for Tea*. The badges can be pinned onto a jacket or bag or even a scarf.

Practice example

This is a good activity to use with children who have experienced loss and possibly placement movements and may be feeling isolated. I have used it and seen moods lifting when the child realises how many people he is connected to. I have encouraged children to show their beads to people they have chosen a bead for. In one case a teacher admired it and invited the child to lead a small group of girls in making their own necklaces at lunchtime. This helped to strengthen her friendship group. It gave her an excuse to call her previous carer and gave her a focal point to start a conversation with her mother during supervised contact (her relationship with her mother was very strained). When I asked her some months later if she still had her necklace, she said in a surprised voice, 'Of course. It's under my pillow now. I need to make another one though, 'cos I got lots more people now.'

My other memorable use of this was with a younger child. She had a limited number of people in her life but I wanted to help her see that there were people who liked/knew her. She loved the beads and became very enthusiastic. She named a bead for her hamster, the dinner lady and the 'lollipop' lady. She also put a bead on for the old lady she waved to each day when she went with her nana to visit one of her nana's friends. She seemed to have a real wish to connect with this lady and with a little bit of investigative work I found that the lady was living in a residential unit. To cut a long story short, I organised for this little girl and her nana to visit the lady who turned out to be a retired headteacher. They formed a friendship and in turn the little girl was introduced to the lady's own grandchildren. She had a whole new network of friends. She felt so important when she went into the residential unit and made Christmas cards for *all* the residents. That was three years ago and she is still visiting. The experience has allowed her to feel valued and to practise her social skills, and has helped her to become a competent and sociable youngster.

Happy Meals
Purpose

- To find out if the child can identify things that make him happy and if not, to help him do this. This can help in care planning. For example, if the child identified that playing football for his team made him happy, you would ensure this was part of the care plan and perhaps also try to increase his opportunity to play football.

- To help a child begin to think of what he can do to feel better. This teaches coping skills and builds resilience.

This is a really good activity to do with parents and children together:

- When used in this way it will increase family members' knowledge of each other and in particular may help parents to understand (or remind them of) what the child needs from them emotionally.

- It provides an assessment opportunity in terms of observing the level of empathy the parent has for the child.

- Used with children over the age of five, it can give them clear ideas of what they can do to please their parent. A word of caution here: parents will tend to write things like, 'Sam behaving makes me happy.' This is unhelpful as it is unspecific. 'I am happy when Sam sits quietly beside me to watch "The Simpsons"', provides the child with an achievable goal. Focusing on the positive and giving praise will usually increase that behaviour. Explain and prepare the parent prior to doing the exercise.

Before continuing with the instructions needed for this activity, it may make it clearer if I explain how the activity came to be created and how I have used it.

My friend's child's hamster died and at ten years old she was able to understand that she wouldn't see the pet again, so she was feeling very sad. I asked if she would like to spend some time with me and gave her the choice of what she would like to do.

Somewhat to my surprise she asked to go to a drive-through fast-food outlet for a Happy Meal. This was something she had never done before. I went with her choice and we sat in the car eating the meal. When she had finished she declared, 'I'm disappointed. The Happy Meal didn't make me happy.' This opened up conversation about how different things make different people happy and how her sad feelings would probably be around for a while as she had loved her pet hamster, but it would get easier with time. There were a few tears and I decided it would be good to try to focus on happy thoughts. Fortunately I had my work bag with me, so I brought out stickers and pens.

'Come on. Let's try to make a real Happy Meal. One that is all yours and no one else's.'

This got a weak smile.

'Right, if this wasn't cola but something that makes you really happy, what would it be?'

'Planting seeds with granddad.'

This made us laugh, and I wrote 'a cup full of granddad' on a sticker and stuck it to the cup. Then, holding up the burger box, I asked the same question.

This brought, 'A day at the safari park.'

More laughter and we stuck another sticker on.

I held up the empty French fries packet, 'And this?'

She asked for paper and proceeded to draw and cut out French fries and write all her friends' names on them to make 'a portion of friends'.

We carried on until we ran out of all the bits of the meal she had ordered, which included making a paper burger, tomato and bun. Before we left the restaurant, I asked for three more sets of unused packaging, which surprised the assistant but she happily gave them to me.

On returning home my young friend showed her Happy Meal to her family and they all made one. The children's Happy Meals (the things they had identified made them happy) became real surprise treats for birthdays, etc. over the following months.

Following this, my friend asked me to do the same activity for a group of 11- to 14-year-olds she worked with. A large majority of them became absorbed in the activity and we created a display of their Happy Meals in the youth centre. I have subsequently used it with three families. It created enlightening conversations and highlighted the lack of positive focus in one family's life. The third time I used it I included the foster carers, mother and children just before the children were to be returned home. From this session we created a star chart where the reward was to choose something from the Happy Meal for the adult to make happen. Happy things were easy to accommodate and included such things as 'a slice of watching a DVD in bed' and 'a cupful of taking Max (dog) for a walk'.

WHAT YOU NEED TO MAKE YOUR OWN HAPPY MEALS

- Fast-food packaging such as drinking straws, burger boxes, chip/French fry containers, paper cup with tissue in it.
- Two circles of brown and yellow sponge to simulate a burger roll.
- Cardboard lettuce (empty cereal boxes are the right weight of cardboard for this).
- Cardboard burger.
- Cardboard tomatoes.
- Cardboard chips/French fries (lots of them).

You will need enough to give each participant one set of the above. Also have:

- Plain white stickers.
- Pens.

What to do

1. Explain that we are going to make a very special kind of Happy Meal. We won't be able to eat it but it will be fun.

   'To get started we need to think of a time when we were happy. Take a moment to think. It may have lasted only a few minutes or maybe even a few days.'

2. Talk together and share the happy memories and then say, 'Now let's make a Happy Meal.' In the same way as I described my first

Happy Meal, engage the child/children/family in thinking about what makes them happy and make it fun by creating 'a dollop of…', 'a cupful of…', 'a wedge of…' and so on. At the end you will have placed stickers with happy-making activities on the food items: 'a slice of play' written on the tomato, 'a dollop of dad' written on the mayonnaise, 'a box of friends' on the French fries/chips and so on.

3. Now you can play with your Happy Meal. If the child handed his mother 'the cupful of love', could his mother give him a cuddle? If the mother is absent, maybe she could send a teddy with a hug, or draw a heart. 'A dollop of dad' might mean arranging a meeting or telephone call. The Happy Meal could help us work out what would make a happy day for the child. Help the parent or carers plan and facilitate this.

A word of advice: do not tell the child that if he makes a Happy Meal you will definitely use his ideas to give him a happy day or a reward – a Happy Meal that included a trip to the moon, buying a puppy or a holiday to Disneyland is unlikely to materialise. It is no less valid, however, as dreaming and imaging these things can be fun and even comforting; it is just not something, perhaps, that most parents/ carers or social workers could turn into reality.

Safe Hands
Purpose

- To help you find out from a child the people in his world whom he feels can keep him safe.

What you need

- Lots of paper, at least A4 size.
- Good quality felt tips.
- Baby wipes or access to a wash basin.
- A safe space to work in (this could be your car; if so, I recommend you use a lap tray or, if the weather is good, the body of your car).
- A friendly and playful presentation.

What to do

Most children I meet like coloured pens. It is important that they all work and are of nice quality. From a child's perspective, especially if they are unhappy or stressed, if their favourite colour of pen is not working it can tip the balance from this being a fun thing to do, to something they are only doing because you have asked them to. It is also important to use nice, clean paper. We are asking a child to produce something for us. Let us then respect their efforts by giving them good materials. Children *do* notice and so do any professionals you may later show their work to.

1. To begin, allow free play. Enjoy the pens and paper, talk about the colours and make your own picture. It is important to join in as this promotes a feeling of togetherness and gives you common ground. Try and draw patterns or simple things the child could easily draw. I tend to do balloons and balls. If you produce too adult or impressive pictures, the child will tend to be inhibited in his work or become more interested in your pictures. What you want is free flowing and relaxed art production from the young person.

2. The next step is to introduce the idea of drawing round each other's hands. You need to judge the point when the production of pictures is decreasing but the child has not yet got fed up with the pens. Introduce it with playfulness and enthusiasm. You might say, with a smile on your face and excitement in your voice,

    > 'Hey! I've got a good idea. Let's draw around each others' hands.'

    I've never had a child say no. By this time I have built up my communication with the child; he has experienced me as a safe, helpful and fun adult, so now he is happy to meet my need to direct the play. Hence the importance of free play at the start. Don't ever be tempted to skip that stage – it is essential.

3. Suggest that the child draws round your hand first. This gives the message, 'I trust you.' It also feels safer for the child. Remember that he might not trust adults and/or be dealing with trauma, so drawing round hands is initiating physical contact. This is a big

deal for some children, so go gently. Once your hand is drawn you could say:

> 'You know, when I was a little girl people used to hold my hand when we crossed the road to keep me safe.'

All you are doing is introducing the idea of safe adults. You may find at this point the child will initiate conversation about safely crossing roads or other safety precautions. If you do, great. Go with it.

4. Then draw around the child's hand. Have as much fun as possible and give lots of compliments. Maybe do a couple of drawing round hands. You will need to judge how much the child is enjoying it and the right time to make the next step. 'I know, we could write the names of the people who keep us safe on the fingers of the hands. That would be pretty cool!'

    Offer to write on behalf of the child. Writing can be viewed as hard work for some children and you don't want them to disengage. You could ask who he likes to hold hands with when watching a scary bit on television. Or at the dentist's, crossing the road, and so on. Remember to ask about a variety of settings. Maybe granny is the safest person in his life but she is housebound and can't hold hands crossing the road. Your assessment will only be as good as the opportunities you give, so give it thought.

    > 'Okay, which finger will we give that person? Which colour will we use to write their name?'

5. To finish up, go back to free play/drawing at the end of the session. Have a tidy up ritual (out come the baby wipes, an opportunity for you to offer help and care) and during this, talk about the safe hand picture, how interesting it is. It will help you to learn about his family. Then ask permission to keep it for a little while. If you are in the office, the child will usually really enjoy coming to the photocopier with you and seeing his work copied. He will usually be delighted if you give him a photocopy to take away. If you are going to attach this to the back of a report, think about waiting to ask his permission at the next session.

Memory Questions
Purpose

- Used for relationship building and assessment.

What you need

- A quiet space where you won't be interrupted.

- A table or floor space.

- A set of question cards – I have made my own and they include the following questions/statements: 'I wish…', 'People like me because…', 'It's scary when…' (see Appendix II for a longer list that can be photocopied, but also add your own ideas).

What to do

Before you begin work with the child, check through the cards and remove any that you feel would be inappropriate. It is rare for me to have to remove any, but the one I most commonly leave out is, 'Being at home is…' I leave it out when children are accommodated away from home and have no contact with their home. (Please note that I am specifically referring to their home and not family members. This widens the subject, allowing precious personal possessions, friends, special spaces, pets and wider community and family to be considered.) Instead I use a card that says, 'When I was at home it was…'

1. Shuffle the cards and lay them face down on the table. Explain to the child that on the cards there are sentences that need to be completed. You will take it in turns to lift a card up and complete the sentence.

2. When you complete a sentence you get to keep that card. *But* if you don't want to complete that sentence you can put the card back face down and try to remember where it is so you don't lift it again. The other player may lift and complete it. The aim of the game is to collect as many cards as possible, and the winner is the person with the most cards at the end.

3. Towards the end of the game there may be a couple of cards on the table that neither party wants to answer. That's fine. Just leave them out. They are 'lost cards'.

Practice example

These cards can lead to lots of discussion. What at first glance seems to be a simple game often becomes an opportunity for the child to feel heard and talk about some sensitive subjects. It's important to use your person-centred counselling skills during this game, and to maintain confidentiality as long as it's safe to do so. If you can't, be clear about this. Give the child reasons and tell them who you will need to speak to and why. Then explain what is likely to happen. How you explain this and the level of detail will obviously depend on the child's developmental stage.

One example of using this game was with a 15-year-old boy who was accommodated away from home. I had only just become his social worker and was told that he wouldn't engage well, didn't speak about himself easily and generally wanted any social work appointment to end before it had begun. The staff invited me to use the small living room, which was where social workers or other visitors met with the young people. It was a nice room, well appointed and very comfortable. However, I politely refused as I was aware that he might associate this room with previous social work visits and probably had some preconceived ideas about what to expect. I wanted to change the setting (remember that rooms have meanings), so I asked if I could use the dining room. This was ideal as it had a table and I could use this as a logical reason for swapping the room. Many children I work with are hyper-vigilant as a result of living with poor attachments to their caregivers and will often question any behaviour, especially new behaviour, from an unfamiliar adult – understandably, as this is an attempt to keep safe.

By the time my young man arrived, I had already set the cards out on the table.

'Hi my name's Audrey. Want to play a game with me?' I said brightly.

No verbal reply, but he sat down beside me. The staff member who had brought him into the room gave me a double thumbs up, a big smile and mouthed 'Progress'.

I explained the game. 'By the way you know that I am your new social worker, don't you?'

Young person: 'Yeah.'

Me: 'Good. Right, let's start. I will go first.'

I deliberately displayed a positive expectation that he would join in. Children sometimes play the roles that are given to them and this child had a reputation for non-cooperation and aggression. I went first as I wanted to demonstrate how to play. I hoped this might ease any anxiety he had.

Young person: 'I could fucking head butt you.'

Me: 'So you could, but come on let's play this. Which card are you going to have? Oh, by the way, please don't swear.'

He chose a card. It said, 'You can help me by...' He added 'Getting me out of here but that'll no happen.'

Me: 'I can do that – get you out of here. It's just that we need to sort things out first.'

This immediately caught his interest and for the first time I got direct eye contact. I could have elaborated at that point. This young man was 15 years old and due to his often very aggressive behaviour it was unlikely he could remain in the unit after his 16th birthday. In fact, keeping the place until he was 16 would be quite a challenge in itself. So one of my tasks was to work out an exit plan.

I chose not to get into that discussion at that point but to continue with the game. I knew it would be easy to come back to in a number of ways and I felt that we could do a bit more warming up before tackling it. I also wanted him to invest in our relationship and give him the chance to pull me back to discussing this subject. In order to feel safe this boy needed to feel he was in control. He also operated around creating confrontation with carers. My hypothesis was that he felt most at ease when he had led people to a place where he could create confrontation and gain control. I was quite deliberately giving him this opportunity in a safe way. I had answered his question honestly but given him an answer he wasn't expecting. I focused on the big long-term plan. Another worker may have replied in the opposite, and they would have been focusing on short-term plans and setting boundaries. If working from a behavioural perspective, their answers would also have been honest.

He chose to carry on the game for a good few minutes before declaring,

'Right that's it. I am not playing.' I noted the lack of swear words and smiled to myself. Perhaps he could be more respectful and engaged than he was given credit for.

'Oh', I emphasised disappointment in my voice.

Young person: 'Well, we're no playing. You're going to talk to me about getting out of here.'

Me: 'You want me to talk to you about plans for you leaving here?'

Young person: 'Aye. Do it. Tell me.'

Me: 'Of course we can talk about that, but from now I want a nicer attitude. Deal?'

Young person: 'Aye. Okay sorry.'

In the above confrontation and power play, the important thing was to allow the confrontation to happen in a safe and controlled way but still remain in control. I kept it low key, but consistent and firm in a way any caring adult should. This creates a feeling of safety and reliability in the relationship. This technique takes practice, but it is essentially about making a good initial assessment, using empathy to understand and value the emotional place your client is coming from and how this translates to behaviour, then holding that behaviour, as opposed to fearing it or trying to avoid it. Ultimately you look to change it little by little, in small steps.

We discussed his exit plan and through this identified things he liked about the unit and why he would like to stay until he was 16. He was, in fact, very positive about the staff, his room, the food and most aspects of daily life. I expect that the 'Get me out of here' statement was linked to fear of rejection and was his way of saying 'I will reject you before you reject me.' I therefore reminded him that he could stay longer than just his 16th birthday and also that he wouldn't get rid of the staff when he was 16 even if he didn't live there. By the end of the session he was smiling, giving me 'high fives' and promising to curtail his setting off the fire alarm and chair-throwing activities.

The next week I went back, I found him waiting in the car park for me to arrive. I had brought several different activities with me but before I was out of the car he asked enthusiastically if we were going to play the cards again. I asked if he would like to. He replied, 'May as well. Now't else to do.'

The second session went well and again the cards led us into an interesting chat about his history, when he talked about the reasons he was accommodated and reflected on the many losses he had had. In further sessions, at his request, we began to do life story work. His behaviour, while far from perfect, improved. His need to confront and risk-take decreased. Staff became more positive about him and he was gradually more able to openly show warmth for them. He remained in the unit and we didn't have the 'Get me out of here' conversation again.

In My Garden
Purpose

- To help a child name family members/people he lives with and begin to talk about his qualities, roles and relationships within the family. This can be a very useful assessment tool.

What you need

- A picture of a garden drawn on a large piece of paper – A3 or flipchart paper is good. This needs to be done before you meet the child and will be a resource you can use many times, especially if you laminate it. If you are not an artist, simple lines to represent the following features will work well or you could cut out and stick on pictures from magazines:
  - A sun – to suggest a happy or warm place.
  - A dark cloud – to suggest a sad place or feeling angry.
  - A play area – I use a swing (hanging from the branch of a tree) because most children like them. They can be soothing because of the rhythm or exhilarating and exciting. Also it is a play thing that adults often engage in with a child.

Figure 8.8: My Garden

- A place with potential danger – I use a garden shed as it may have sharp things inside and lots of corners for things to lurk in.

- A magical place or item – this gives potential for children to use their imagination and for anything to happen. I use a fairy/elf hidden behind a door in a tree trunk.

- A wise creature – I use an owl perched on a branch of the tree. In folk traditions and fairy tales owls are often portrayed as wise creatures, so they may be familiar to some children already.

- A pet – I put a cat in the tree. Pets are often important to children and can be their best friends. Also studies have shown a correlation between abuse and neglect of animals and of children living in the same home, and their play may reveal this.

- Hiding/scary places – I make a flap to lift up the grass to reveal soil, worms etc. This provides the possibility of people being 'buried', for example, one little girl drew her gran who had died and placed her under the grass.

- White card or paper.

- Coloured card.

- A glue stick.

- Coloured pens – make sure they are good quality and working, and easy (thick or with flat sides) for a child's hand to hold.

What to do

1. This is the rapport-building stage so begin with free play, drawing pictures together and having fun talking about favourite colours and so on. Give compliments about the child's drawing. Never ask, 'What's that?' This can be a real put-down if the child feels he has made a good representation of something. Instead ask, 'Can you tell me more about your drawing?' or, 'I really like this part. Can you explain it a bit more to me please?' The aim of this stage is to help the child relax, especially important if it is your first meeting, but also because you are about to talk about family, which may be a difficult thing for the child to do. It is very common for me to come across children who have been severely warned not to talk about their home and family.

2. In your own drawing, begin to draw simple people. By this I mean mimic a child's drawing ability because if you appear too competent it can put the child off drawing his own pictures (I find this especially true in the eight and above age group).

   The child often asks, 'Who's that?' which gives me the opportunity to introduce the idea of drawing family, 'Oh, that's my brother and this is my mum. Hey! I've got a cool idea. Do you think you could draw your family and/or the people who live in your house? Because if you do that I've got a fun activity we could do with the drawings.' This should be said with excitement and enthusiasm. If the child doesn't give you the opener by asking who you are drawing, ask, 'Can I show you my picture?' and follow with introducing your family and the cool idea, as above.

3. Once the family pictures are drawn, cut around the individual people and if you have time, mount them on coloured card. The purpose of this is to emphasise their value, make them special and create a resource you may use again. You can ask the child to choose the colour of the card for each person, 'What colour would dad like?' This is a gentle introduction to talking about the people as individuals.

4. Once your people pictures are made and ready to use, bring out your picture of the garden. Talk through the picture first and then let the child explore under the flaps. Does it look like a garden they have been to? Would they like to play in the garden? Where would they like to be in the picture?

   At this point encourage the child to place the picture of themselves where they would like to be in the picture. A lot of children choose the swing. What does it feel like to be on that swing? Did they go high? Did anyone give them a push? Who?

5. Try to get a conversation going between you, letting the child lead as much as possible. Keep your tone of voice and expression interested. Be careful not to push, as the child may not be ready to tell you any more and that is okay. This is not always easy, but speaking as a social worker who is always aware of child protection issues and usually only working with children where there are significant concerns, it can be a real discipline not to push for more. It is very important not to pressure any child. Go gently, build up trust, show you are interested and attentive, and the child will tell you in his own time more about his life and any worries he may have. If you push, you become an unsafe adult. By this I mean that at the very least you will close down communication; at worst you may cause the child emotional harm.

6. When you have finished talking about the child in the picture, suggest adding someone else – who is going to be next to join you in the garden? Again, get the conversation going as to where the child may go and why. Invite the child to add other family members and try some questions such as 'What does Billy do when mum is sitting in the chair?' As the cast of people join the picture, check back with the child, 'Are you still on the swing?'

This is because the child may want to move to be nearer or further from one family member as the story unfolds.

'What do you think Billy is saying to nana?' is the sort of question that can lead the child into free play, acting out a story line. If this happens, don't interrupt, just watch and listen. This could be imaginary play or it could be the re-enactment of a real situation. If it is a real situation there is likely to be a lot of detail. The child's play may depict actions more associated with an adult or may use words that do not fit his own vocabulary and there may be strong emotions. Either way, in my experience children do depict scenes from life, but remember, they are very much in the here and now. So if he depicts his mother as being very angry, it may be they had a row that day. Tomorrow his mother may be depicted as very caring. The important thing is to look for recurring themes as you work with the child over a period of time. It is my belief that themes that are consistent over time often give a more accurate representation of how the child experiences that person. It could also be an indicator that the child is trying to understand or make sense of a particular situation by replaying it repeatedly, or externalising the feelings associated with it. However, it is worth bearing in mind that if the child consistently represents his mother as angry, it could be that his mother *is* always angry, but equally it could be that the child is always anticipating his mother's anger. Both would give cause for concern as they are having a significant effect on the child's emotional health and *may* indicate risk, but both are clearly different and the cause different.

Working with the child is, in my opinion, one of the most important ways to assess a family's situation and to work out your plan of intervention. But it must be done in conjunction with assessment of the adults involved and considered in conjunction with information from other agencies, otherwise your assessment will be incomplete and inaccurate.

7. Once you have completed this activity (either because play itself has naturally ended or time is running out – remember to give a child timed warnings to tidy up – ten minutes, five minutes, tidy up time!) you need to decide with the child what you are going to do with his family member pictures. Have a plastic envelope ready to keep them in if you are entrusted with them. You might

suggest that next time you laminate them to make them last longer. One little boy kept his laminated family in his pocket and later in the drawer beside his bed. He showed them to people and when angry, sometimes stamped on them.

8. In further sessions you could use the family members to do a genogram/family tree.

Practice example

The concerns for Emma (age ten) were around parental drug misuse and neglect. When I first met her she was angry and aggressive and told me in no uncertain terms that she didn't like social workers, she wasn't going into care and I could 'F-off.'

I sat down. 'Do you like drawing, Emma?' (I had been told that she did.)

'No. I hate it.'

I said that was a shame as I had heard that she was very good at drawing and so I had brought my very good pens that I usually only kept at home, because I thought that as she was good at drawing she would know how to use them. I pulled out a big case of pens from my bag in a variety of shades, and I went on to say that I had also brought special paper that was only really for artists. I set them on the table and out of the corner of my eye I could see that she was interested. Then I said, 'Of course I asked the wrong question didn't I? I asked if you liked drawing, not if you were good at it. You can be good at things and not like doing them. So, I wonder if I asked you, "Emma, would you like to do some drawing with my special pens and paper because you are good at it?" what would you say?'

At this point I was avoiding eye contact and pretending to talk to myself. Emma was edging towards the table.

I continued, 'Ah well, best not to ask. Probably not fair to ask you because you said you don't like social workers. I don't want to upset you because I like you and, well...maybe I'll just put them away and think again.'

Emma interrupted, 'No. Ask me! Ask me!'

At this point I made eye contact, 'Are you sure?'

Emma: 'Yes, I like you, I think, but mum said I'm not allowed to like f...ing social workers.'

Me: 'Okay, I'll ask you but only one more time. Emma would you like to draw with my special things?'

Emma: 'Yes. Can I use the red pen?'

And so Emma and I drew for about half an hour and we talked about colours and different kinds of materials. We agreed I should come back next week and I explained that next week I would like her to do an activity with me with the pens and then I would mount some of the pictures she had made, so she could take them as presents for friends or family. She was delighted.

Just before I left I established with her that I would speak to her nicely and I expected her to speak nicely to me. She said, 'You mean I've no to tell you to f-off or say you are an f…ing social worker?' I smiled and agreed that was my meaning. 'Oh, and I'll no hurt you neither', she added.

I smiled, 'That's a good rule – no hurting neither.' Emma left the room, only to shout and swear at the headteacher.

The next week I brought the pens and some card out and we did free drawing for about five minutes. I drew some figures and she asked who they were. I explained I was drawing friends and family. Could she do that? 'Aye, I could,' but she carried on drawing animals and flowers. She has a mischievous grin on her face. I smiled inwardly. This youngster had me sussed. So I took a tack I don't often take:

Me: 'Okay, we both know the deal here, don't we? I am a social worker and social workers like to talk about life with you and your family, right?'

Emma: 'Aye, I ken [know].'

Me: 'How do you feel about that?'

Emma: 'It's okay, but ma family's a f…ing mess.'

Me: 'You're telling me you understand why I am here and it's okay to talk about your family, but you feel your family is in a bit of a muddle?'

Emma: 'Aye.'

Me: 'I don't know your family. Could you draw them so you can introduce them to me? I would really like to get to know you all better to see if I could help with the muddles.'

Emma drew all her family members in meticulous detail. As she drew them she told me little bits about them. We ended the session as we ran out of time. Fortunately I was able to go back the next day and we used the In My Garden activity.

Emma placed her father figure in the shed. She stated she wasn't allowed in there.

She placed her mother beside the mushroom and elf because she 'takes stuff and it makes her see things.' She placed her gran on the deckchair beside the food with her baby sister, because her gran looked after them a lot. She placed herself on the swing, but then moved herself quickly to the black cloud saying she was sad because she wanted a normal family.

We had a very open conversation about the lack of food available and general emotional and physical neglect. Emma and her siblings are now placed with their grandmother.

Chapter 9

Emotional Literacy Activities

Children learn social and emotional behaviour from their carers. These are essential skills not only to help them understand and advocate for their own needs but also to help them engage positively in society. Carers who have their own vulnerabilities may not be able to teach these skills to their children and there is therefore a role for helping adults to do this work.

Mr Mad, Mr Sad and Mr Glad
Purpose

- To provide opportunities to name and talk about emotions.

What you need

- Three cardboard boxes the same size and shape. Empty laundry-tablet boxes are ideal.
- Simple drawings of three characters, Mr Mad, Mr Sad and Mr Glad. Stick the boxes to the tummy area, so that the head and arms stick out and can be seen, as in Figure 9.1.
- Pens and small pieces of paper.

Figure 9.1: Mr Mad, Mr Sad and Mr Glad

What to do

1. Make the box characters with the child and while you are doing this talk about what the names mean. For instance, mad means angry or frustrated, etc. Explain that when the characters are made, it will be the child's job to fill up the tummy (see below).

2. If you are planning to do this activity in a residential or nursery setting, the character boxes can be given a permanent home on a table, on top of a bookcase or pinned to a wall. I carry them around with me as I am always on the move. The next step is to invite people to write or draw something that made them mad, sad or glad that day and put it in the tummy (box). We then review together what is in the tummy, creating discussion about emotions. In a residential or other setting we might do this every few days and I have found it works best in groups.

'You and Me' Jars
Purpose

- To help children find out from their positive role models (people they look up to) how *they* deal with strong feelings.

What you need

- A selection of jars decorated by the child you are working with. The decoration should include the word of the emotion the child wants to find out about.

What to do

1. While decorating the jars, decide with the child which emotions she wants to find out about. This tends to be the emotion the child is struggling with. Most typically it is anger, as the children we work with tend to get into trouble at school because of how they express their anger. But bear in mind that anger is a secondary emotion, so you also want jars that represent sad, happy, scared, etc.

   At this point also find out from the child which adults in her life she looks up to or admires. Teaching staff, foster carers, social workers, football coaches and youth workers are all people who are easily accessible and usually willing to help.

2. Take the jars to the people the child has named and maybe also some others you feel would be appropriate, but explain what you are doing. Ask them to write on a piece of paper what they do when they are mad, sad, happy, etc. Fold the paper up and pop it in the jar. They do not need to put their name on it.

   Check what people have written, just in case there is anything unsuitable or not clear. It isn't likely but it is not uncommon to have to print what they have written on the other side if the writing is difficult to read.

3. At the next meeting give the child the jars. You will have a really interesting time opening all the notes and reading out what people have written. This will give the child a valuable resource to keep of positive ideas of how to deal with strong emotions.

TIPS

If you have any concern about how safe it would be to use jars, you can use boxes or plastic containers. I used jars with some of my more sensible and quiet teenagers. They enjoyed using glass paint to decorate. One young girl put them on her windowsill so they became a very colourful feature in her bedroom, especially when the light shone through.

Balloons That Go Pop!

Purpose

- I use this when working with young people who are behaving in a way that might jeopardise something in their life, for example, a school placement or their freedom. This activity is to try to give a visual image of the loss that could occur if the young person made a wrong choice.

What you need

- A balloon inflated as big as it will go (you are going to write on it, so it needs to be hard).

- A black felt-tip pen.

- A pin.

What to do

1. With the young person identify what is at stake if she carries on with her negative and challenging behaviour. For instance, she may lose a school placement. Now help her think about the positive things about school she would miss. This can be a challenge, but there will be something. One of my children said 'Getting water from the water machine' and another was 'Being able to buy chips at lunchtime.' As the adult, remind them of things like missing out on learning opportunities, friendships and so on. Write these onto the balloon and really make a big deal of them, how important they are and how good the balloon looks when it is inflated.

2. Invite the young person to burst the balloon. If you have inflated it until it is really hard, hopefully it will burst into pieces. Look at the balloon on the floor and express sadness and disappointment at losing the beautiful balloon and along with it the school opportunities, etc.

   Be aware that a common reaction from children is to laugh and say 'So what?' or that they don't care. Don't be put off or feel this has had no impact. The reactions are defence mechanisms and show that you have made an impact.

Angry Balloons

Purpose

- To assist an older child to control anger.

What you need

- A balloon.

- One-to-one adult support.

Note that balloons used this way can be dangerous and I wouldn't use this activity with children who are developmentally under the age of 13. I always use this activity with an adult supporting, but make your own judgement as each child is different.

What to do

1. When the child is calm and relaxed, talk to her about anger. Ask what happens when she is angry. How does her body feel? Practice taking deep breaths in, holding that breath and then slowly releasing it. Does she feel tension leaving her body? You can also try making a fist, holding it tight and then letting go. Tense and then relax. Explain that when are angry we get tense.

2. Talk about the last time she was angry. What was the cause? Try to tease that out if possible to break down the steps that led to the outburst. If appropriate, share the last time you were angry (remember, nothing too personal), and break down those steps.

3. Take a balloon, blow it up, and for every breath state one of the reasons for your upset feelings:

   Breath 1: 'I was angry with myself for not getting back to the car before I got a parking ticket.'

   Breath 2: 'I was angry that I had allowed myself to be fined, when I could have done lots of other things with that money.'

   And so on.

   Once the balloon is filled with air, explain that all your anger is now in the balloon and you are going to gradually let the air out and so let your anger go.

4. Letting some of the air out, state, 'I forgive myself for getting late back. These things happen.' Carry on until the balloon has deflated.

5. Now comment that you feel better because all your anger has gone. Invite the child to do the same, thinking about the last time she was angry. You will probably have to help the child with the forgiving statements.

6. Do this every time the child has angry outbursts. For some children it will be a very hard thing to do, as it not only requires them to be self-aware but also to own their anger. It may take a long time for the child to be able to talk through her anger and forgiving statements without support. But once she can do this, you can suggest that the next time she gets angry she asks her caregiver for a balloon. Make sure that you have previously talked this through with the caregiver and have their agreement that they can provide a balloon and support/supervise the child if she asks for a balloon.

7. Instead of shouting, swearing, acting out, etc. suggest the child gives her anger to the balloon. Emphasise how impressive this would be and also the positive consequences of this. If she does follow this through, offer lots of praise.

Balloons to Carry Messages
Purpose

- To initiate conversation around what we would say to those people we no longer see or have access to (perhaps because they have died, gone missing, are in prison or are no longer seen following adoption).

What you need

- Balloons, or if you prefer, paper Chinese lanterns.
- Pens.
- A quiet outdoor area.
- A story about wind taking messages (optional).

What to do

1. Have a conversation about what the child (and perhaps you too) would like to say to the absent person. Suggest that maybe the wind could carry this message to the person.

2. Write or draw the message on the balloon and then send it off by either just letting it go, or tying a string on the end and releasing it when the wind tugs it. Ask the child which way she would prefer to do it.

Hide the Faces

Purpose

- This is a small-group activity to help developmentally very young children identify emotions and talk about feelings. It can also work in a parents' group, helping them to understand the value of emotional literacy for their children. They may even like to make a set of cards for the children to play at home.

What you need

- Lots of picture cards with line drawings of a face showing one each of three emotions: happy, sad, angry. Have a number of cards for each emotion. If drawing them yourself sounds too daunting, check out old magazines or clip art images on the internet (making sure they do not have copyright restrictions) and then photocopy and laminate them. Or copy the template given in Appendix X.

What to do

1. Hide the cards around the room, having kept a sample of each face.

2. Show the children the first face card, 'This is a sad face. See the tears and the sad mouth.' Explain you are going to say 'Ready, steady, go' and on 'Go' they have to search and find all the sad faces until you say 'Stop'. They will then bring all the cards they have found and you can see who has the most 'sad face' cards.

While you are counting talk about what makes people sad. Ask whether they can show you what it looks like when they are sad.

3. Repeat the game until you have done the three emotions.

4. As an extension of this game once they have learned how to play it, or for older children, you could make cards that represent situations that might arouse that emotion (see Appendix VIII):

   - Card showing a birthday cake: happy.

   - Card showing a child snatching a toy: angry because another child took my teddy.

   - Card showing a balloon escaping: sad because I lost my balloon.

5. Introduce and talk through all the situations represented on the cards, talking also about the emotion attached to that situation. Show the face card that matches and then send the children off to find as many situation cards to match the face card as they can. To begin, have only one type of situation card for each face card, so, for example, you would have numerous birthday cake cards hidden around the room to match with the happy face. However, to extend this further, especially with older children, make up numerous situation cards that could match a happy face: a present, a child laughing on a swing, a dog wagging its tail and so on. Similarly for the sad face: a child with a cut on her knee, a child crying having dropped an ice cream, etc. Do this for the angry face as well.

   This requires the children to really think about what the picture represents and helps them begin to recognise and name emotions.

Changing Faces
Purpose

   - To help children understand that people have a range of emotions.

This activity may take several sessions as it involves making and decorating masks, a fun activity in itself.

What you need

- Blank face masks – found in craft shops, although paper plates and elastic thread will do.

- Pens or paints.

- Glue.

- Stickers.

- Feathers.

- Bits of material.

- Tissue paper.

- Cotton wool and a variety of materials to decorate masks.

What to do

1. Together with the child name as many emotions you can think of and then make a mask for each emotion, decorating the mask according to the emotion. For example, you may paint the 'sad' mask blue and stick tears on. This is just a suggestion – let the child lead as long as you both recognise the emotion:

   Me: 'Can you help me to understand why we need to paint the mask an angry pink?'

   Child: ''Cos I always get annoyed with my doll 'cos her pink dress won't go on.'

2. Once all the masks are decorated and dry (this may go over more than one session), pile them on top of each other, with the emotion you are feeling at that moment on top. Hold this mask up to your face and explain, 'You see we can wear all these masks in a day because right now I am showing you the happy one, but if someone suddenly said something unkind to me I would put the sad face on and hide the happy one.'

3. Practice the idea with the child relating it to herself and to you in your current situation or a shared recent experience. Play with the masks together and from here (with older children) you can go on to explore how we sometimes tell the world we are happy, sad or angry but we are actually feeling something different.

Promise Cards

Purpose

- To generate discussion around promises.

- To give the worker an opportunity to find out more about the child and her world.

What you need

- Coloured card.

- Glue stick.

- Good-quality felt-tip pens.

- Folder.

- Stickers (optional).

- Some blank promise cards (made prior to meeting the child). Take one piece of coloured A4 card and cut it in half. Stick one half in the centre of another piece of A4 card in a contrasting colour, so as it looks a bit like a picture frame. You now have a blank promise card. Make lots the same and place them in a folder. Presentation is key so give these cards high importance by making them special right from the start.

What to do

1. Start a discussion about promises, maybe by giving the child an example that you can both remember (e.g. 'Remember I promised I would visit you at home? I did that yesterday so I kept my promise'). It helps if, before using this activity, you have been able to create a number of situations where promises have been made and kept. Invite the child to tell you promises that have been made to her and kept or not kept and how she felt about that.

2. At a point that feels right (maybe the flow of the conversation is slowing), suggest with enthusiasm that you make the child a promise right now and you have something very special with you – blank promise cards!

3. Take the promise cards out of your bag. Invite the child to choose one, maybe in her favourite colour. Then looking at the child, but holding the card in your hand, make your promise. Some of the promises I have made are:

- I promise to read you a story at the end of each of our sessions.

- I promise to listen to what you say and try to understand, but you might need to help me understand sometimes!

- I promise to do my best to make sure you are safe and happy.

- I promise to give your cat a tickle behind his ears next time I visit your house.

- I promise that each time I meet you we will work hard but we will always have a little bit of fun, for example, I might sing you a silly song or tell you a joke!

4. Once you have made your promise, write it down at the top of the card and draw a picture that represents it underneath. Then, taking great care and emphasising that this is a special and important card, decorate the border (draw a pattern or use stickers, etc.).

5. Present, in a serious way, the promise card to the child and say the promise out loud again. Sometimes I hold the child's hand as I do this. Do whatever you want, but make it a memorable moment.

6. Now invite the child to make some promise cards. At this point many of the children I work with have already asked to make one or declared that they are going to. If this happens, that's great, just go with the flow at the pace the child wishes. Try not to put parameters on who they might be for, because if you said, 'Why don't you make a promise card for someone who is special to you?' you could inadvertently exclude the child from making angry promises. In my own experience of doing this, it is very common for the child to use this opportunity to vent anger, with promises of violence being not uncommon. ('I promise to chop off your head', a nine-year-old's promise to a bully. 'I promise to cut you up into pieces', an eleven-year-old's to his father, turned out to be a fairly innocuous reference to a computer game he played with his father, so be sure you check out the meaning and

context of promises.) When presented with these, I reflect back to the child the feeling content of the promise she has made and accept the angry feeling as valid.

If the angry feeling is directed at a real person, I would attempt to talk this through and deal with the upset. Sometimes the child is not in the right place emotionally to do it at that point, so I would suggest that we need to think a bit before we give angry promises out, and that I will keep them until next time. I usually try to ensure that I see the child again quickly if this happens, and emphasise to her that her promise is important and that's why I will come back soon. On my return I work with the child around feelings. If she is still angry with the person and still wish to give the person the card and we have explored what the possible consequences of giving it might be, I would facilitate this in a planned and safe way, using conflict resolution techniques. This situation sometimes requires intensive support for both parties after the giving of the card. You may need to pull in a network of people to help, for example, teachers, carers, community police and supportive family members.

To date I have not had a situation where I thought the child's safety would be compromised. In fact, the opposite is usually achieved because it is about being angry in a safe and controlled way. However, if my judgement was that it would be unsafe to give the card, I would tell the child that I will not allow her to give the card to that person at this time, because to d so would be unsafe. However, I would keep the card safe for her and together with other people (naming who these people will be), I would try to improve the child's safety in the hope that one day it would be safe enough for her to give that person the card, if she still wanted to. You could make a promise card conveying this message.

7. As children are generally experts on their own situations, I use this opportunity to ask them for ideas about what the adults need to do to help their situation. Be careful, however, not to dismiss what, at first hearing, may sound fantastical and unrealistic.

For example, when I was asking a boy of nine what he thought I needed to do to protect him, he stated 'Build a dungeon at my house so I can put her in there when she is doing her bad drinking stuff and I can go to nan's.' What he had identified was that he needed his mum in a contained space so that she was safe and he needed to go and stay with his nan.

8. If the promises made are positive ones, encourage the child to give them to the appropriate person that day. The giving out of positive promises usually brings a lot of good attention for the child and can become quite addictive. One of the children I worked with was a prolific promise-giver, but struggled to follow through, however. We therefore needed to revisit the exercise, reinforcing the idea that you only give a promise you can keep.

9. If you are near a photocopier, you could ask the child if she would like a copy of the promise. Most children are delighted at this prospect and it gives you the opportunity, having gained the child's consent, to make a copy for your records. You can, with the child's permission, use these in reports as a practical representation of the child's views/wishes, but do this with caution. Don't take the content out of context.

10. The next time you see the child, review how it felt to give out the promises. What were people's reactions? Did anyone make them a promise in return? You could use role-play here. Play the role of the child and she can teach/show you how she gave the promise and she can show you how people reacted by role-playing the other person. It is often very useful to gain feedback this way when children have limited descriptive language or limited concentration (or both), and also it is often just more fun. Ask if the child has begun to fulfil any of her promises and whether she would like to make any more.

Safety Shields

Purpose

- To help a child to develop an internal coping mechanism when faced with an upsetting situation. This has been a useful tool with children who are being bullied or verbally abused.

What you need

- A story that illustrates the use of shields. I use *I Fought at Bannockburn* (Ross 2001). For some children the text is too long and complex, but the important part is the pictures that illustrate the use of shields.

- A flat piece of cardboard – a shop will usually be happy to give old packaging.

- Scissors.

- A roll of tinfoil.

- A glue stick.

- A4 white paper.

- Good-quality colour pens.

What to do

1. Look at the book with the child and talk about how the people are using their shields. How strong the shields must be! How do you think the people behind the shields might be feeling? Look together at the pictures on the shields and discuss their meaning.

2. Lead the conversation on to when the child might find a shield handy to have. Children will usually talk about fights and think in a concrete way. You will need to introduce the idea of a shield that could protect your emotions. Your conversation with the child could run like this:

    Child: 'I could use it to fight with.'

    Adult: 'Yes you could, just like in the story. What if it was a magic shield that nobody else could see but you? Could you hold it up to protect you?'

    Child: 'That would be so cool!'

    Adult: 'Yes it would be cool because then you could use it anywhere to protect you when people said nasty things to you and hurt your feelings. What do you think?'

    Child: 'Mmm.'

    Adult: 'I know, let's make a magic shield, it will be so cool.' (Said with enthusiasm and fun.)

3. Help the child to draw out a shield shape on the cardboard to fit her size and cut this out. Apply glue and then cover with tin foil.

4. Admire this shield. Hold it up in front of the child. Wonder aloud if it is strong enough. Lead the conversation on to how to make it

stronger. Talk about a time when someone has said a nasty thing to you and to protect yourself you thought of all the things you liked doing and that made you feel good. That was you using your magic shield that nobody else could see and it was very strong.

5. Help the child to think about the things in her life that she enjoys or that make her feel good. If possible, help her to think of people who she trusts and feels safe with.

   'I know if we drew these things and stuck them on your shield they would make it strong.'

6. Admire the shield. Be really over the top and use lots of exclamations. This is very important because memory is helped by association with sensory experience, so different sounds and facial expressions or movements associated with different pictures on the shield will help the child to remember the pictures. For example, for one picture you might give them a high five; for another you may say, 'Wow!'; for a third you may clap and so on.

7. When this is done, play a game where you ask the child to close her eyes and to describe her shield. You might need to help and prompt. Really celebrate all the details she remembers (the important thing is she should be successful). She doesn't need to remember them all and if she is struggling, you should end the game:

   'You are so clever you remembered two of your pictures with no peeking. Wow! It must be a really strong magical shield because there is a picture of it in your head. Now if you practise lots and lots that picture will get really strong and your magic shield will start to work. Then when someone says something to upset you, you can see your magic shield and it will protect you.'

8. Decide with the child where she is going to pin up her shield to practise remembering it. I often suggest we pin it on the wall beside the child's bed, so she can see it before going to sleep. This is useful if nightmares are an issue. One of the little girls I work with uses her shield when she wakes up after a nightmare or when she hears her parents arguing when she is in bed.

9. Ask the child if she would like to show her carer her shield and maybe help the carer make her own one or help a sibling make

one. I encourage this as it reinforces the process, but it is always the child's decision.

Roll the Feelings Dice

Purpose

- To increase emotional literacy by helping the child develop awareness of facial expressions and body language and how this has an impact on others.

This game can be played one-to-one with a child by making some adjustments, but it works better with small groups of two to three children, like a sibling group. It can also be very effective when used with family groups including parents.

What you need

- A dice that has pictures of faces depicting different emotions (I made my own one).
- A grid for each player with the six faces with different expressions that depict different emotions on it (again, I had to make my own).
- A tub of counters (you can buy these in toy shops).
- A small mirror.
- A kitchen timer.
- A place to play that offers some space to move around in.

What to do

1. Give each player a 'feelings' grid.
2. Look at the grid and the dice and identify the feelings that are depicted. The grid could have the names of the feeling written under each face, but don't miss out on the discussion as it is a warm-up exercise as well as testing literacy. This is also the time when each player, with the help of the game leader, identifies

their 'golden feeling'. This could be a feeling that the child says she feels a lot or a feeling that she struggles to express. As the leader you help them decide. Explain the 'golden feeling' will help them gain points later (see below). You could play one game where golden feelings are ones you feel a lot and one game where the golden feeling is one you find hard to express (or each player could be different). For your own sanity, leaders keep a note!

3. Explain that everyone will take a turn at rolling the dice but you have to roll it in secret as the other players are not to see which face you got. You will let the game leader (who is usually the adult in charge, but not always) see the dice. This is to make sure no one cheats and to allow you to have a whispered conversation if you need help.

4. Set the timer for how long you wish the game to last (for small groups of young children I suggest 10–15 minutes. You can play it twice if they are having fun. In larger groups, family groups or with young people I suggest 20–25 minutes). The first player rolls the dice secretly, shows the leader, and then using facial and body language, acts out the emotion.

5. The other players have to guess the emotion. You can invite the player who is acting out the emotion to look in the mirror to check that she thinks she is depicting the emotion accurately. If the other players are struggling to guess they can ask one question each, for example, 'Can you tell us a time when you felt like that?'

6. The leader and the player who is acting the emotion tell the other players as soon as one of them names the emotion correctly. If it is taking a long time or just not working, help by perhaps giving examples of when someone may feel that way. Make sure your examples are very simple and obvious. It is likely that a lot of the people playing will have emotional literacy difficulties (at least this is true of the client group I work with), and they will find this game challenging. For example, if I wanted people to guess 'sad' I might say, 'A boy loved his dad very much. They went everywhere together. The dad took good care of the boy and they had lots of fun together but one day the dad died. The little boy cried and cried because he was feeling very...'

7. The other players are then invited to award the acting player counters or points. I have found it is good to have a structure to decide how many points are given and why. To keep things

simple and fair (depending on the players' abilities) you can either decide at the start of the game how points are awarded, which is what I prefer to do, or give prepared guidance on how to award points. A suggested structure would be: one point (counter) for good effort; two points if the acting player used lots of expression and body language; three points if everybody found it easy to guess the emotion. I tend to point out that it is in the other players' best interests to guess quickly as it means they will get more turns as the kitchen timer is ticking away.

8. Players place their points or counters on their grid in the correct place, so if they acted out sad and got two counters they would place these on the sad face. If they roll the dice next time and it lands on sad they miss a go unless it's their 'golden feeling', in which case they can act it out again in a bid to win more points.

9. The next player rolls the dice and repeats as above.

10. The game ends when the timer goes off (but let the person acting finish their turn). The person who wins is the one with the most counters.

Practice example

The time I have found this game most successful is when working with family groups, especially where violence has been a feature.

One family of four children under 12, with parents in their twenties, had reports of domestic abuse. Children talked of loud arguments and of their father hitting their mother. During the playing of this game, when the father showed a sad expression, both the mother and children guessed he was portraying anger. It was a revelation to the father that he looked angry, and we spent considerable time together after the session deciphering different feelings and body language. The father was devastated to learn through conversation during the game (I had stopped the timer to allow for this) that his family considered him to be an angry person. It also became clear that the children read any expression of emotion by either parent as an angry emotion. Misreading emotional cues is linked to the impact on the emotional brain of living with anxiety and fear and is not uncommon in children we work with (Ratey 2001; Schore 1994). These children are constantly on the alert for perceived danger, and can misinterpret facial expressions, which explains children who blow up in the classroom for no apparent reason.

This gave me an opportunity to discuss with the parents the impact of their loud verbal arguments. The couple agreed to couple counselling as well as a series of measures around protecting the children from further emotional harm. In the next planned session with the children, I played the game with them just as a sibling group. They were clearly more comfortable with this and recognised a range of emotions. We spoke about how much they had helped their mother and father last time and that their mother and father were going to get help to 'tame their angry feelings' so that they could be angry without being scary and without hurting others.

I continued to work with the girls individually and as a sibling group, developing a supportive and nurturing relationship. This enabled further emotional literacy work to be done and also work around raising their self-esteem. I also continued to visit the family together. At the end of six months the parents had finished their couple counselling, within which time they had briefly looked at anger management. We played this game as a whole family group and there was a marked difference in everybody's ability to engage and communicate easily.

Another example is with a teenage boy. I used this game with him as a 'Getting to know you' exercise as we had just met. After playing this game he said to me, 'I don't know how to do "happy" Audrey. I mean I knew when we were playing to smile and that, but I don't ever feel happy, just angry and sad. I don't ever remember really feeling happy.' This young man had undiagnosed depression. He had been in foster care for a number of years, but nobody had done life-story work with him and so his past was unresolved. In a bid to protect himself he had forgotten chunks of his life. Once his depression was being clinically treated, we embarked on a journey of discovery together, unfolding his life story at a gentle pace. He is 17 now and in full-time employment and he tells me he feels happy.

SIMPLER VERSION OF THE GAME FOR THE DEVELOPMENTALLY
YOUNG OR YOUNG CHILDREN (PRE-SCHOOL)

What you need

- A dice with faces on it depicting sad, happy and angry, each emotion occupying two sides of the dice.

- A board for each player with three faces depicting sad, happy, angry.

- Three pieces of coloured card for each board, the right size and shape to cover one of the faces on the board.

What to do

1. The youngest player rolls the dice. She identifies the emotion on the dice, if necessary with some help from game leader.

2. The player then has to make a face that conveys the emotion – perhaps looking in the mirror to see if she likes the face she has made.

3. The other players clap and the player covers, with a piece of card, the face she has just imitated.

4. The winner is the player who covers all her faces first.

Emotional Lotto

Purpose

- A game for developmentally very young children (three and above) to learn about emotions and to name them correctly.

What you need

- An A4 (or larger) piece of paper divided into six sections with simple faces depicting emotions drawn in each section (see Appendix X). I call this the 'board' from now on. I only use three emotions, happy, sad and angry, using each picture twice on the board. This is because it is aimed at younger children.

You can make bigger boards for older children with a wider range of emotions. Each player/child has their own board, so make as many as you need. If possible draw them in different colours.

- For each board you will need six cards, two with happy faces, two with sad faces and two with angry faces. These should be the same size as the sections on the board and drawn in matching colours, that is, the red board will have red cards.

What to do

1. Give each player a board. You can have as many players as you have boards, but very young children have short attention spans, so the fewer the players the better in that case.

2. Help the children to look at and understand the boards. Hold up a happy face card and ask who can point to a happy face on their board. Do the same with the other two emotion cards.

3. Next shuffle the cards so that all the colours are mixed up, and place the cards face down on the table.

4. Invite the first child to pick up a card. Can she name the emotion? If not, help by giving the word.

5. Is it the right colour for her board? If yes, the child places it over the matching picture on the board. The aim of the game is to be the first to cover the board with the matching pictures.

6. If the card does not match, the child lays it down in the same space and players try to remember where the cards are, introducing elements of a memory game.

I made this game up to use as an assessment tool when I was working with a seven-year-old girl who didn't seem able to name emotions. She was very vulnerable and I wanted to gauge her understanding so that I knew how to engage her in play and conversation about what was going on at home. She enjoyed the game and I discovered that she could indeed name emotions, but could not apply these to situations – she could recognise and name a sad face but couldn't tell me what would make her or any of her family or friends sad.

At that point I was not sure if that was because she did not have the cognitive ability or perhaps didn't feel safe enough to talk about feelings. I found out that her teachers, whom she knew better than me, were having the same problem. She appeared happy and relaxed in my company and at school, but appearances can be deceptive. So for this child I extended the activity.

EXTENDING THE ACTIVITY
What you need

- The same board.

- New cards. On these I drew simple stick figures to represent a scene that may evoke one of the emotions, for example a child being given a present (happy); a child being told off (angry); a child loosing their balloon (sad) (see Appendix VIII).

- A dice with the six sides covered in pictures of faces representing the three emotions, happy, sad, angry. You will have to make your own (see *Roll the Feelings Dice* activity on pp.156–60).

What to do

1. Give each player a board.
2. Place the cards on the table, face up this time.
3. Each player has a turn to roll the dice. When the dice stops, the player has to name the emotion uppermost on the dice and then find the situation card that evokes that emotion and place it on the board in the right place.

Practice example

The same little girl found this game very challenging. She believed all the situations represented angry. I was not surprised by this as in her home, angry was a safe emotion. The health visitor, the school teachers and I all experienced anger from the family at the point of engagement. The result of this was that the family had become quite skilled at deflecting services. In short, it could be frightening for professional adults to be in the home, so what must it have felt like for young children? The result was that visits and meeting were kept very brief and the child was left with angry and aggressive behaviour, no friends and the label 'a challenging child'.

I worked with the parents in the home, bearing in mind safe practice precautions. Initially it was just me hanging on in there in the face of hostile behaviour. Eventually we got past this and forged an excellent working relationship. Anger is a form of defence and these parents lacked confidence and self-esteem and were very afraid of authority. Once we got past this they were able to accept support and I continued to work with the child on emotional literacy. This required a lot of repetition, praise and new opportunities, reinforced by the school staff – good communication between us was essential.

EMOTIONAL LOTTO WITH PLAYDOUGH

Children don't want to play the same games every week so I developed this to use with playdough (see the recipe in Appendix I). The strength of this version is in the fun of doing it more than the results.

1. Play the game the same way up to matching and naming the emotions. Then ask the child to make a model out of the playdough of something that makes her feel the emotion she has matched.

2. Keep going until everyone has three models. The children need time to make the models and to chat about them.

3. If you need to reclaim the playdough, take a photograph of the models and post a copy to each child. Children love to get something in the post and this will help build your relationship

with them. If it is home-made playdough, you can let them take it away with them.

This activity can lead to building up a shoe box of emotional literacy items and perhaps onto making comfort boxes (see below).

Comfort Boxes
Purpose

- To give a child/young person (or an adult) an activity that helps to soothe them when feeling vulnerable or stressed.

What you need

- Pens and paper (optional).
- Time to take the child shopping and a small budget.
- A selection of small boxes and/or tins (discarded boxes and tins which held biscuits, chocolates, etc.).
- A safe, private space.

What to do

1. In a quiet and safe space, sit with the child and talk through the fact that everybody, no matter who they are, gets upset sometimes. Using people she knows, or even characters in a film or story that the child is familiar with, think of examples together. Extend this into what that person or character does if they are upset, then gradually begin to talk about what the child does.

   Some of the things the child talks about might be self-sabotaging. One young lad told me he smashed windows. I needed to lead the conversation into talking about what he got from that and why he thought it helped. For this child there were two answers: the physical release of pent-up energy and a feeling of closeness to his father as he remembered this was what his dad had done when he was stressed.

   Some children will find it very hard to name what they do; in fact, they may be at a stage where they scream, yell, cry or act out and have not as yet developed strategies to find comfort more acceptable to their age and context.

2. This is the purpose of the comfort box. For those unable to name
    what they do, you will need to help. Ask someone who knows
    the child well for their observations of the child, but you should
    also have an awareness of the child's general likes and interests
    to draw on.

3. Together with the child, work out what brings comfort, relief
    or good feelings. At this point you may want to use pens and
    paper to write these things down or draw them. Once you have
    achieved this you can move to making up the comfort box.

4. Invite the child to choose a box from your selection. She might
    change it later if she finds an item won't fit in or she finds her
    own container, but it helps to have a tangible box at the start.

    One of the little girls I worked with loved *The Sound of Music*
    and of course there is the song in which Maria sings about things
    she does when feeling sad. We made up a comfort box full of the
    favourite things and sang the song endlessly. In the song, Maria
    likes 'raindrops on roses' (we used a silk rose with a silicone
    raindrop), 'whiskers on kittens' (we put in a photograph of a
    kitten), bright copper kettles (we included a kettle from a doll's
    house), and warm woollen mittens.

    This helped a very young child to grasp the concept of what
    a comfort box was and how to use it. Gradually, with the help of
    her carer, the little girl was able to identify her own comforting
    things. One of those was her nana. Her nana, however, had died
    and there were no photographs, or possessions. I therefore got
    her to tell me about her nana and carefully recorded this for her.
    The little girl was unable to read independently so I recorded it
    on a tape. I also asked the care home staff if the girl's nana had
    used a particular fragrance. She hadn't, but they did tell me that
    her nana's breath was often garlicky, as she liked to chew cloves
    of garlic. I therefore played a sensory game with the child where
    I asked her to smell a variety of things with eyes closed and to
    tell me what they were. I included garlic, which she named with
    surprise and excitement, 'That's nana!' so we included garlic in
    her box. I did this game with her as I did not wish to assume that
    she associated garlic with her nana, and I also wanted to give her
    the joy of discovery if she did, indeed, associate garlic with nana.

TIPS

Before you do this activity, make up a box for yourself. This will help you to get a feel for the process and will also give you an example to share.

Storytelling
Purpose

- Children love stories. When I work with children and young people I not only enjoy, but also find it really helpful to use stories with them. It is a great way to build a relationship with a child. It is a nurturing and enjoyable activity and it can bring a sense of familiarity to a new relationship, by creating a shared experience, and it only takes ten minutes.

Most children learn classic children's stories if not at home, then in nursery or children's centres. So I have learned some of these off by heart and often tell a story the first time I meet a young child. The look of recognition and sometimes surprise is a real joy to see. It is also an important opportunity to give the message, 'I like what you like. I am familiar with one aspect of your world. I do and like similar things to the other safe adults in your world.'

This is just the beginning to using stories. I often make them up for children. This might be sparked by a conversation or a situation that has arisen. Once a young person I worked with was given a teddy bear from a number of toys donated to social workers to give away to children. She commented that as a child in care she sometimes felt a bit like a teddy bear in a charity shop. This young person had been permanently placed with foster carers and her siblings were either also in permanent care or adopted. This opened up a conversation about her situation on the way home in my car.

Following on from this I wrote a story to capture the conversation we had had in the car, to let her know that I had listened and valued it. It was also a fun thing to do and I thought she would enjoy the playful aspect of it. It gave me a way of trying again to do some life-story work with her. She had previously been highly resistant and stressed when I suggested it.

She loved the story and showed it to her teachers, her foster carer and she also added to the story. In essence, we began her life story work by writing teddy's life-story together. This was the start of us discussing her life story starting with the present, which is usually the safest place to begin.

A colleague then approached me and asked if I could think of any way to help a little girl who was going to have an unexpected change of placement. The child was seven years old and very anxious about the move. I wrote the story of 'Alfie' for her, incorporating some of the child's own circumstances:

The fairy brought Alfie a kitten home to care for as he was so badly neglected.

Alfie wanted to keep the kitten but was only allowed to keep him for a little while.

There was an unexpected and sudden change that caused strong emotion.

The kitten was kept safe through this, even though it had to go to a new home.

The rescuer (the fairy) was always in the background and helped to keep the kitten safe, while also sometimes having to bring upsetting news.

My colleague read the story to the girl and she told me it soon became the child's favourite book. She carried it everywhere with her and found it very difficult to part with, even for the shortest time (e.g. to let her social worker photocopy it). I later made up 'Alfie's play box' to give her the opportunity to extend the story into her play and thus let her take control of the characters and what happened to them. The play box contained dolls that represented the fairy and Alfie, a toy cat and a scene from the story.

I am not a talented story writer, but it isn't necessary to be in order to make up and use stories to help children and young people.

In my box of toys I have a feely bag specifically made up with items that lend themselves to storytelling. I change it fairly often, but currently I have in the bag a magic wand, some coins, a gold cup, a small teddy, a ghost toy and a few figures. I use the bag as I would a feely bag (see the *Feely Bag* activity on pp.172–76), and then invite the child to make up a story using all or some of the items.

Some children find this quite difficult. They may not have had much opportunity to play or may never have been relaxed enough to get to that stage in play where they get absorbed in their own imagination (typical of children with poor attachments, when all their energies go into maintaining a state of alertness to possible or perceived dangers). Sometimes it could be lack of confidence in themselves or fear of getting it wrong. For all these children, helping them to make up a story and tell it, and for that story to be enthusiastically received and praised can be highly beneficial to their emotional development.

For other children, the opposite may be true. They use their imagination to retreat from reality when the world becomes too much and they find making up stories easy. Playing together with the storytelling bag gives the opportunity to get into a discussion about this coping mechanism.

Practice example

I worked with an eight-year-old who found the storytelling bag very easy and she kept me enthralled with countless stories. There was nothing alarming or even very special about these. They were the kind of stories I would expect to hear from most eight-year-olds, but what was notable was the fluency and quantity. I commented on this, saying, 'You are very good at making up stories. You seem to be very quick at it. I have not met anyone before who can make up such good stories so quickly. Can you tell me about that?' She told me that she did it all the time. When she couldn't do her work at school she would stare at one spot on the window or on her desk and tell herself a story. She went on to say that when she was at home no one spoke to her. So she lay face down on the sofa, burrowing her face into the corner where all her imaginary teddy bears lived. She explained they were about the height of her thumb and marched around under the cushions in a world of their own. She was never lonely or afraid. She would just take herself into her teddies' world.

In time I helped her to tell her grandmother, who was her safe adult, about her teddies' world. This alerted her to how alone this child felt when at home and her grandmother made concerted efforts to change the situation. Eventually the child went to live with her.

This storytelling bag frequently leads to discussions around ghosts and nightmares and difficult bedtimes. Using the ghost model and some of his own toys, a seven-year-old played out a recurring nightmare he was having. It transpired he had been watching a lot of videos for older viewers. We were able to play out a new story using a magic wand to make it into a silly ghost who could only throw candyfloss at people. We replayed this story repeatedly and he told it to his foster carer, teacher and friends. While he still woke with the nightmare, he learned how to cope with it, and once awake, was less distressed.

Puppets and Furry Friends

Purpose

- Puppets can offer a safe way to communicate in a non-direct and unthreatening way.

Many of the children I work with find it very difficult to express how they feel in an accurate and appropriate manner. Some recognise one or two feelings they are comfortable with and present these regardless of the situation. Most childcare workers in social services will have met a child who is most comfortable expressing anger or child who consistently smiles and gets on with whatever life throws at them.

Some children need to project their feelings onto toys or pets before they can own them. One little boy I worked with perceived himself as a bad boy (this was unsurprising as he was developmentally at the stage where he believed he was responsible for everything that happened in his world – the 'magical thinking' stage of development). As he was recovering from physical and emotional abuse it is no wonder he believed himself to be bad. After all, good boys are not assaulted by their parents regularly, are they? But his dog, his constant companion, was a good dog. If the little boy was ever complimented on anything, he would inevitably attribute his success to his dog. So using puppets was perfect for him as they allowed him to tell his story whilst retaining some emotional distance, until he was able to own the feelings. With this little boy I also used his dog in a similar way to how I use puppets. I only introduced puppets in settings where his dog was not available.

Puppets appeal to the senses, particularly sight, touch and sometimes sound, and so are an accessible tool that often appeals to the most distressed child/young person. Sensory experience is strongly linked to the attachment process, and distress can also cause regression to an earlier developmental stage. In the hands of a skilled and sensitive operator, puppets can take on personality traits all of their own. These can be tailored to meet a child's unmet need, so the puppet could, for example, be another playmate or nurture figure for a child who has very few people to nurture her. The puppet could mimic an aspect of the child's behaviour that is undesirable or unsociable by asking the child to help correct this in the puppet. You, in effect, provide the opportunity for the child to problem solve as to how to change her own behaviour. At the very least you are increasing her awareness of how it feels to be around that behaviour.

But, most importantly, puppets are fun! Thus the child is rewarded for communicating with you (and the puppet) and so is more likely to stay engaged.

What you need

- Puppets.

- A good dash of self-confidence.

- A sense of good fun.

- An ability to play imaginatively.

Think carefully about the puppets you use. What kind and how many? There is no right or wrong answer here. You can buy some beautiful puppets or you could make your own from a paper bag or an old sock. What you need to consider is what is right for you – your puppet is an extension of you, your co-worker if you like. I am not very confident in my puppetry skills so I tend to buy some really nice puppets. I find that this helps me because they are very appealing, and because I like them I find it easier to create their personalities and play with them. It's important that you are comfortable, relaxed and enjoying the puppets, because if not, the children will not be either. Children are very astute and quickly tune into adults' emotional states.

I favour having a variety of puppets to hand. This is because if the child wants to tell her story through puppets, she will generally look for a number of characters to represent her experiences, feelings or in some cases, the other people involved in her life. There is an argument here for the majority of your puppets being handmade, as this can create scope for you to support the child to make her own set of puppets to tell her own story. I tend to have at least a few handmade puppets available and art material at the ready so we can create a character not found in the collection offered.

You may also wish to have a chair at hand that the child can hide behind, so she can operate the puppet while out of sight, as would happen in a puppet theatre.

TIPS

As previously noted, I have a number of puppets but I only have three that act as co-workers. These puppets travel in my car and go wherever I go. The reasons I have three are:

- I can only create and consistently portray three different puppet personalities. It is important the puppets present as consistent characters, so I need to be confident I can achieve this. Consistency provides a sense of safety.

- I need three because at times I want to tell a story and this gives me my main characters.

- Sometimes I need the puppets to have a dialogue between each other. Three is a good number to demonstrate friendship dynamics and conflict resolutions.

- I make the choice to lend my puppets (as transitional objects) to children when they are in distress. They can be a real comfort and offer the child an opportunity to practice how to 'tell Audrey' using the puppet. The down side is that I still need a special puppet the other children are familiar with to act as my co-worker. So having three affords me the ability to do this, as one puppet that has been lent to a child is explained away to other children as being on holiday or off sick, which children readily accept.

Treat your puppets with respect. By this I mean when you have finished using them, gently place them in your bag or down on the floor. If you are promoting them as personalities then you must follow this through or else the role you are trying to create for the puppet becomes insincere, and will limit your puppet work. Would you throw a friend to the floor or stuff them in a bag?

You are not trying to be a ventriloquist, so don't set yourself up to fail.

Children will often look for their favourite puppet, so have the same ones available consistently and if, like me, you choose to lend them out, remember at the start of your work to let it be known that other children play with the puppets too. In this way, when one puppet is 'on holiday' and it happens to be a favourite one, it does not come as too much of a shock that it is not there for the child who is looking for it. I have prepared some photographs with each of the puppets in holiday locations such as the beach or in a caravan, and made these into postcards to send to children when they miss a favourite puppet. These postcards are often held in high esteem, well worth the mild embarrassment felt when posing the puppet and taking the picture.

If you intend to lend them out, buy two, just in case one goes astray and it happens to be important to another child. I know it's potentially expensive, but it is worth while.

Young children find it harder to manipulate puppets. Have some that are designed to fit smaller hands.

I like to choose puppets that have places to hide things in. For example, my rabbit puppet has lettuce leaves that open out. My elf has bags and pockets. This gives me scope to hide a compliment card or a card with a question on it and very occasionally a sweet, all of which come from the puppet, not me, of course.

Feely Bags
Purpose

- These are soft drawstring bags in which small objects/toys are placed. Traditional feely bags are used to engage children in sensory activities. They should have at least five different objects in them, one that stimulates each sense. These are some ideas, but the possibilities are endless:

  ○ Touch: feather, stone, fir cone, bubble wrap, shiny paper, sandpaper.

  ○ Taste: sugar cubes, sweets, stock cubes, box of raisins, carrots.

- ○ Smell: soap, material soaked in perfume, scented eraser, small box with tissue sprinkled with a food essence flavour, some spices placed in a small box.

- ○ Sound: bell, crispy paper, squeaky toys, musical instruments, small sealed bottle with pasta shapes in it.

- ○ Sight: a bottle of bubbles, string of beads, mirror, wind-up toy, book.

These bags are great for working on children's sensory experience. You can use them one-to-one or in a group.

What to do

1. Invite the child to place her hand in the bag and choose an object without looking. Younger children will need to be allowed to pull the object out instantly to look at it, play with it and talk about it. Make the activity interesting and exciting by the use of voice intonation and facial expression.

2. With older children, see if they can guess what they have in their hand before they pull it out. Can they describe what it feels like?

3. This game helps strengthen your relationship with the child because it is fun and requires the development of trust. Once the child has pulled all the objects out, she can hold the bag and it's your turn to put your hand in, which you do with the same excitement, sense of fun and also trepidation.

USING FEELY BAGS FOR EMOTIONAL LITERACY WORK

Having used the more traditional feely bags as a fun activity to develop my relationship with a child, to provide the child with sensory experience and me with opportunities to assess her development, I have also extended this activity into emotional literacy work by filling a feely bag with things that lead us to talk about emotions. So we have a cat soft toy that I have stuck felt tears onto, a brave soldier, a shy puppet, a scary monster and a happy cow that moos because this makes people laugh.

On extracting these objects I encourage the children to name the emotion an object represents, or if they get stuck, I tell them. Then we try to have a chat about that emotion. It may be around why we think the character may be feeling that way, or a time that we felt like that. This is a useful exercise to do as an introduction to emotional literacy. Children generally respond very well, enjoying the familiarity and yet fun element of the feely bag.

Practice example

On visiting a family for the first time I used a traditional feely bag with the four children (all under ten) and their parents. The issues in this family were physical neglect and domestic abuse. Studies show that emotional neglect or abuse is also likely to be present in children raised in this environment. My purpose was relationship building and assessment. At first the father was very reluctant to join in; however, I used humour, encouragement and persistence, almost to the point of insisting that he participate. I believed it was important to do this in order to:

- Establish my authority. I was aware that he used silence and watchfulness as a method of control within the family group and I did not want this to become accepted behaviour when I worked with the family.

- I wanted to ensure that he understood on an emotional level that I wanted to include him in my work in a positive way and recognised him as a valued member of the family group, while not accepting controlling behaviour.

- I believed that there was a possibility that his resistance was down to lack of self-confidence or lack of self-worth and therefore it was important to include him at a point where the task requested of him was easily achievable and relatively undemanding, thus providing him with the opportunity to succeed.

The children loved the fact that their father had put his hand in the feely bag and their response was one of delight and enthusiasm. It rewarded his effort so much so that I met no more resistance from him for the rest of the session. The little girl, aged ten commented, once everyone had had a turn, 'This is like a real family.' On asking her to tell me more about that, she said, 'Well we are all playing and laughing and that.' I asked how that felt, but my question was too direct at that point so she shrugged and moved away. I recognised I had got caught up in my adult agenda by asking that. My motive had been to let the parents hear a very clear statement from their daughter, but it was too soon for her. I used this conversation with the parents later, away from the children, to point out the impact of their behaviour on the children and family life.

At my next home visit, we reused the traditional feely bag with different objects, as everyone had enjoyed it and familiar games build predictability and trust. We began to talk about smells and tastes that reminded us of places, people or experiences. This brought a story from the mother about going swimming as a child, when she smelt the little bit of paper soaked in cleaning fluid, and a story from dad about his granny hitting him for getting his clothes sticky when he ate an orange (having pulled out a tangerine from the bag and my asking him to open it and share it). The children were attentive to their parents and brought their own stories. I introduced the emotional feely bag and again the children and parents engaged easily, but this time our conversation broached more sensitive areas. One of the girls pulled out the cat and she handed it to her father and said, 'I get sad when you and mum fight.' The youngest child got the brave soldier and she wanted to keep it (which of course I allowed, as I have spare ones) "Cos they had to be brave all the time.' When her father asked why, she stated "Cos it's scary here at night.' Her mother dismissed this notion, but a sibling interrupted, 'It's scary 'cos you can get hurt.'

The parents were quite closed to their children's communication. They laughed, dismissed comments and turned away. I responded by affirming/reflecting back what the children said and commented directly to the children, 'You are doing really well. You are working hard and trying to help mum and dad. Mum and dad are struggling a wee bit. They need Audrey to help them to listen.' I then provided the children with occupational play in the form of playdough in their room on a mat on the floor. I worked with the parents asking them to be proud of their children and to think about what they had said. I explained it would be good parenting and I would be impressed if they accepted their children's feedback without getting angry with them. I explained we would end the session and meet in a couple days. I then went through and played with the children. Following this, I called the children's school and asked them to monitor the children closely for any signs of stress or upset. I also made a point of seeing the children in school prior to my next appointment with the parents. They gave no indication that anything untoward had happened at home but I am always aware that increasing a child's ability to directly feed back to a parent can, at least in the initial stages, increase risk to them from parental reaction to this work.

Chapter 10

Explaining Things Activities

We, as adults, hold more power than we realise. If we are not aware of this it becomes too easy to do things to children without fully explaining the reasons and consequences of our actions. This is even more worrying for children in the magical thinking stage of development when they believe they are responsible for what happens to and around them. It is therefore essential that we prioritise time to explain to children what is going to happen and why, taking into consideration their developmental stage and finding activities that help the process. Some examples of such activities are provided below.

DNA Water

Purpose

I developed this in response to the need to explain to an eight-year-old child what a DNA test was and why it needed to be done. The child, like many vulnerable children, was developmentally younger than her age. I have used it on a number of occasions since.

DNA testing is potentially a very sensitive subject, but is becoming a more frequent occurrence, especially in social work practice. This activity is purely to help explain the DNA test itself, as children often experience things being done to them or requested of them without adequate explanation. There is no attempt here to replicate the science of DNA except in the most simplistic way.

What you need

- Four clear bottles (representing the child, mother and two possible fathers; more bottles are needed if there are more men involved).

- Four pieces of paper.

- Felt-tip pens.

- Three plastic jugs of water.

- Food colouring – yellow, blue and red.

- One empty glass with the child's name on it.

What to do
BEFORE THE CHILD ARRIVES

1. Draw pictures to represent each person – the child, mother and two fathers. If the child is old enough to read, place names on the pictures and stick them onto the four bottles. If you are not a confident drawer, a clear identifying feature will do (colour and style of hair, glasses, beard, male/female clothing, etc.).

2. Make up three jugs of coloured water, one yellow, one blue, one red.

WHEN THE CHILD ARRIVES

1. After a general chat and introduction of what you are going to talk about, explain to the child:

    'We all have something special inside us and it is called DNA. It's special because everybody's DNA is a little bit different – isn't that clever?

    There is something else about DNA that is really cool. Your birth mum and your dad each gave you a little bit of each of their DNA when they made you. That's really special, isn't it?

    The only people who can see DNA are very clever doctors and when they look at your DNA they can see a bit of your mum's in there and also they can see a bit of your dad's DNA.

    It's hard work to understand all that isn't it? Let's see if I can show you.'

2. Now look at the prepared bottles, each with a picture representing those involved in the test, and ask the child to pick out the one that looks a bit like him. As you proceed, punctuate your instructions with lots of affirmation: 'Wow! Well done! That's good!' etc.

'Now, do you think you can pour some of the yellow water into your bottle? We are going to pretend that the yellow water is your DNA. Can you now pour some of the yellow water into mum's bottle? We know your mum has yellow DNA because you grew in her tummy. She is your tummy mummy.'

3. Ask the child to pour a little of each of the remaining colours into the other two bottles – a bit of red in Adam's and a bit of blue in Keith's.

'We have two bottles left. One is Adam's and one is Keith's and mummy is not sure if Adam or Keith helped make you.
But the clever thing is that your DNA can tell us!
Now, who will you pick to go first? Adam? Right, pour some of the water from Adam's bottle into yours. Oh! Look what has happened!'

The child will see that the water has changed colour to orange and you enjoy the moment together.

'So, if it was Adam who helped make you, your DNA will be orange because it is a little bit of mum's yellow DNA with a little bit of Adam's red DNA. Cool huh?
But remember, mummy's not sure it was Adam. It could be Keith, so let's do the same thing with Keith's bottle. First we need to put this orange DNA into the glass.' (with the child's name on it, prepared beforehand)

Put it on one side.

'Now, put a bit of mummy's DNA from her bottle into yours again, because we know you have got some of mummy's DNA because you grew in her tummy.
Good. Now you can pour some of Keith's blue DNA into your bottle. What's happened?'

The water will be green and you can ask, 'Can you tell me what that means? Yes, it would mean Keith helped to make you. Well done! This is hard stuff to understand.'

4. Now explain what is going to happen next in simple straightforward language, along the lines of:

'So what we are going to do is collect some of your real DNA, mum's real DNA and Keith and Adam's real DNA and give it to the clever doctors. They will have a good look at it and then write a letter to tell us which colour DNA you have and then we will know if it is Keith or Adam who helped mummy make you.

Remember I said only special doctors can see your DNA. All we need to do is rub this spongy lolly inside your mouth – you can do it yourself – and then dab it on this special paper. It doesn't hurt. It's just like brushing your teeth.

We'll get mummy to do it first, okay?'

5. At this stage, proceed with the collection of the DNA.

As I said at the beginning, however, this is potentially a very sensitive area, and a bit of preparation beforehand will be needed. This activity just helps to explain the DNA itself and goes no way to looking at the complexity of family relationships or the impact of being given DNA results.

It is also worth planning ahead about how you will answer questions about facts of life, especially if the child is unaware of them. Discuss this with parents beforehand and find out what the child knows and the words and language used to discuss sex and procreation. Perhaps the mother could be present while you do the activity.

Maslow's Boxes
Purpose

- Assessment: this activity helps assess the client's awareness of his or his child's needs. If used with a family group you can observe and assess family dynamics, and possibly also parenting strengths and weaknesses.

- Education: it can help explain human needs and how these relate to development and the effect on development when these are either met or unmet.

- Emotional intelligence: when working with individuals this activity can give a deeper understanding of how the parenting and care they received in childhood have influenced their own development.

How you use the activity will affect which of the above is the most prominent outcome.

What you need

- Seven lidded boxes, each a little smaller than the other so that when stacked they form a pyramid. You may find a set that comes packed together inside the biggest box. Otherwise a variety of small boxes with lids will do, as long as they stack on top of each other in decreasing size. Label each box on its side as follows, starting with the smallest at the top of the pyramid:
  - being all you can be (self-actualisation)
  - beauty, nature, balance, order and form (aesthetic need)
  - knowledge, understanding, exploration, curiosity (cognitive needs)
  - respect for self and others, feeling competent, self-esteem (esteem needs)
  - receiving and giving love, affection, trust and acceptance (love and belonging)
  - protection from danger, feeling safe (safety needs)
  - basic needs such as food, drink, shelter, etc. (physical needs) (this is the largest box at the bottom of the pyramid).
- Lots of slips of paper, about 2 inches × 1 inch.
- Fine felt-tip pens.
- A basic knowledge of Maslow's hierarchy of needs (see Gross 2010).
- A confidential and quiet space, preferably with a table or flat surface.
- Enthusiasm – use of self.

What to do

1. Explain that you want to tell the person you are working with all about human needs. It's pretty cool and maybe even exciting once you get the hang of it. Ask the person to help you place the boxes out on the table. With adults and older children you might encourage them at this stage to read the labels on the boxes. With a family where there are small children, see if they can find the smallest box, the largest box, etc. It is important to have as much fun as possible and to engage everyone, so lots of smiles and words of encouragement.

2. Say you want this to be fun but that there is also a serious side to it and a lot of thinking will be needed. Tell them they are going to learn about psychology.

   If I am working with a child or young person, I might say something like, 'I am going to tell you about a very wise man who lived a long time ago. He was curious and clever and fascinated by people. His name was Maslow, and he worked out what people need to grow and develop. Because he was kind he wrote it all down so we could learn to look after ourselves and each other.'

3. Ask everybody you are working with to put the boxes in order of size, starting with the largest box and laying them in a line on the table. Note that it has the label 'Physical needs'. Ask the child to think of all the physical needs we require to keep alive and healthy, write them on the slips of paper and place them in the box. If necessary, the social worker/facilitator can help with writing. See if the child can fill the box. You will need to support discussion around needs with ideas if appropriate. Try to personalise the activity to the client's situation, 'What are your baby's physical needs? What are yours, and are they different? Who made sure your physical needs were met when you were a baby? Do you think your physical needs were met as a baby? Can babies meet their own needs or are they dependent on an adult?' and so on.

4. Repeat the above with all the boxes, and as you go along, place the filled boxes in a tower, starting always with the largest. Engage the youngest children in discussion while the adults and older children write on the slips. Ask them what they need when

their tummy rumbles or what a baby needs when it cries (a child of three and above would manage this question). They may like to draw a picture on a slip and 'post' it in the box.

For assessment purposes note as the boxes were being filled where your clients had the most or the least difficulty.

5. Once the tower is complete (this may take up to an hour, as people often find it challenging) make sure it is balanced well and standing firm. Explain in simple terms Maslow's theory that if one need was not met at the right time, then the next need could not be met properly and so development suffers as a child grows up. This might explain why some children have problems in life.

Keep it relevant. For example, in cases of physical neglect, point to the 'Physical needs' box and explain, 'Your child's physical needs are not being met just now. I know this because when I came yesterday the house was very cold and John had only a nappy on. He was cold to touch and he was crying because he was also hungry. This is what I mean by not meeting his physical needs.'

Be blunt and straightforward but stick to the facts. This is not being insensitive. It is being fair. Clients need to know clearly what the problems are. Sometimes professionals try to soften the blow by using lots of language or by not being direct enough. It is human nature not to want to hear negative messages, and clients either genuinely do not understand what is being said or mentally block more subtle messages, and are then criticised when no changes are made.

6. Allow the client to think for a moment and then to challenge you on this observation if she wishes. Repeat your message, giving another example if appropriate. Be clear and firm but also compassionate and respectful.

7. Once any discussion that arises (if it does) has ended, demonstrate the effects of this. Pull the bottom box (physical needs) away from the pyramid. You could ask the client to do this or it could be a job for the youngest child. Observing the pyramid fall, state, 'That's what is happening to your child's development.' Pause. 'It's falling down. His development is collapsing because his physical needs are not being met.'

There will often be a significant emotional reaction to this. It is a hard message to give and being visual it often touches people in a way that words don't. Distress can be a catalyst for change, so if your client is upset, allow this to happen. Don't try to comfort too soon. Use your own clinical judgement as to how long to allow this stage to last. This may require self-discipline, as some workers find it difficult to contain feelings of sadness or distress and come in too early to meet their own needs, not the client's. When you are ready, with lightness in your voice, say something like, 'Come on. It is not all bad news. Look at this. You can always build the pyramid back up. You can really help your child and we can sort this problem out together.' If a child is involved in the activity, ask him to build the pyramid up again or do it yourself. 'I know you can turn this around. I know you can meet his physical needs and the reason I know this is…' Give some positive feedback based on fact – an observation or a report from another professional, remembering to note even the smallest positive action. 'When I asked you to get your child dressed and give him breakfast, you did that and did it well. I also like the way I've seen you smile and cuddle him. But you need to meet his physical needs and I am here to help you work out how to do what I know you can do. So are you up for working with me on this one?'

8. Depending on the gravity of the situation, you may want to point out here what the consequences would be if the parents continued to fail to meet the child's needs, as you cannot continue to allow these needs to remain unmet.

9. Presuming you do get agreement from the parent to 'build the pyramid back up' and work towards meeting the child's needs, move to the first stage of task-centred practice (Lishman 1991).

Doing the work

1. Agree what the issues are and how they need to be addressed. Name who is responsible for each task, and the timeline of when this should be done. Type/write this up and ask the client to sign the agreement.

2. At this stage you may also consider using scaling to assess the client's confidence and willingness to undertake the task (De

Jong and Berg 2008; Turnell and Edwards 1999; see also *Scales and Scaling*, pp.113–18). This has a way of revealing where obstacles might be and helps the client to think realistically. 'On a scale of 0–10, how confident do you feel that you can (get up early to attend to the baby)? Zero is no confidence, ten is you have no doubts you can do it.' Use the scale the client chooses to elicit more information. 'Ten – wow! That's amazing, especially when you haven't managed to do it before. What gives you that confidence today?' or 'Six, that is pretty confident. What is it that makes you scale at six? What would need to be different (change) for you to move to seven?'

3. The lower levels of the pyramid which cover basic physical needs, education and learning, are easier to break into tasks for parents to work on. As you move higher levels, which cover love and belonging etc., these can be more difficult to break into tasks. However, you will find ways of getting the evidence to show that the parents have at least begun to attempt to meet their children's needs. For example, they could make sure they attend their child's school show or parents' day, offer praise when shown their child's drawing, make a commitment to participate in parent/child play sessions or agree to discuss with you their difficulties in emotionally connecting with their children and work out ways to help change that. Even if this achieves only a small change, resilience studies show that it can have significance in a child's life.

Practice example

This is one of many activities born out of trying to solve a particular problem with a family. I was working with a single parent where there was a high level of neglect, but no other issues like alcohol or drug misuse or mental health problems. On my first home visit I found it difficult to get in the door due to full sacks of rubbish and clothing in huge piles and general household items strewn across the floor. On entering the living room, I found a child sitting on top of a coffee table. I could not see any floor space and couldn't access any of the bedrooms. The bathroom and kitchen were equally cluttered, with the addition of serious hygiene concerns.

The parent agreed to the child staying with a relative while the house was cleared. The child went home when this work was completed. However, it was only a short time before the house was back to its cluttered state, with a risk to the child's health and well-being. The child returned to the relative, but nothing I did seemed to help this young woman to improve the physical environment and care of her child. I felt I needed to help her understand why this was important. I felt I had allowed a situation to develop where she was tidying up for my visits. Indeed, this was confirmed by her child when I used the *Doll's House* activity with her (see pp.97–104). She played at 'Mum', tidying up before my visits. Her play was very detailed, including mimicking me knocking at the door. She used adult words in her play and I felt she was conveying actual events.

Reflecting on this, I decided I needed to move the issue of neglect away from our working relationship into a neutral space. I wanted to empower this young woman to make changes to the child's environment that would last. I had attempted task-centred work, solution-focused techniques and motivational interviewing to no avail. I wondered if she didn't engage well with words as I noticed she was more appreciative of visual experiences. There were many pictures and ornaments around the house, mainly depicting people doing tasks, and I had made a habit of trying to have a few minutes of positive conversation around these objects. She always engaged enthusiastically and showed me details I may have missed.

Out of this, the idea for Maslow's boxes was born. She was visibly upset when I used it with her, and I was encouraged to see this, as previously any discussion about problems had been met with disinterest or a blank stare. At the end of the session she said, 'I get it now,' and there were improvements made in the child's care, sustained for a further six months. Regrettably, I eventually did have to move the child into kinship care, and while this was not the outcome I wanted, at least I know that the mother understood why it had happened and consented to the move, which made the process a better experience for her child.

I have also used this activity with young people (14+) to help them understand their vulnerabilities and behaviour. Using an old social background report written when they were young children, we went through the exercise using the information in the report. The results showed some boxes sparsely filled whilst others were better filled. Together we thought about how it felt for them not to have their needs met and the strategies they used to compensate. One young person was able to recognise that her mother had tried hard to care for her physical needs but due to domestic abuse, she had not been emotionally available. She said, 'So that must be why I feel so empty all the time, because my mum didn't fill my emotional needs box up.' I agreed with her, but critically we were now able to think about how to fill up that box. We looked for people who could help fill it up. She had a good network of caring professionals and she easily began to identify others. To strengthen this, I used the *Candle Work* activity (see pp.187–90) and following this session, her anger decreased towards her mother. She wanted to spend more time with her and I organised nurture sessions to begin to repair the relationship, which had been strained for a long time.

Another young man was very angry with his social workers and the care system since being accommodated away from home as a young child. He felt he should have been left with his birth family. We went through his social background report and related this to Maslow's boxes as well as looking at his current experience of his birth family and helping him to see that behaviours hadn't changed and parental risks were still evident. He began to conclude himself that he could not have remained in his parents' care. This led to him being very sad and experiencing feelings of loss. While this was hard and he needed a lot of support, it was positive because his misplaced anger had made him reject all the support and services on offer. He had been very vulnerable and stuck. Having a better understanding of his history allowed him to accept support and move on, even though this was painful. He is now attending college and successfully maintaining his own home.

Candle Work

Purpose

- To identify the important people in a child's life and to help the child to feel valued and connected to people.

What you need

- Tea-light candles (I buy a big value-bag of white ones).

- Tea-light candles in different colours, as many as possible.

- Matches.

- Tin foil or recycled foil trays.

- A steady table – cover it in the tin foil or lay the trays out on it.

- A space without a smoke alarm and that is not draughty. To be honest, this is the biggest challenge!

If working with a very young child or a child who is very active or has a conduct disorder, you need another adult who has a good relationship with the child to help you keep this activity safe.

What to do

1. Take your candle tin (I use an old biscuit tin) out of your bag and explain to the child that you are going to do something really fun and exciting. Play a guessing game with the child – can the child guess what is in the box? You could give him clues. Most people are fascinated by or enjoy candles, and for children and young people there is a sense of being allowed to do something fun and a little bit risky, which adds to the attraction. Having this kind of introduction to the activity gives an opportunity to set the tone of the session – upbeat, positive and fun.

2. Once you have opened the box or tin explain that you are going to light lots of candles, so many in fact that the room is going to glow and be cosy and warm. Ask the child to help you get the space ready. Put the tin foil over the table or lay baking trays out. While doing this I talk to the child about trust. I emphasise that I only do this with children whom I can trust to listen, to be sensible and to be safe. We push up long sleeves, and tie back long hair. I like to ask everyone who is participating to wash their hands (and possibly wipe their face) before we start. You don't have to do this but I feel it adds to the importance of the occasion and helps the children to feel refreshed and focused.

3. To begin, I ask the child to choose a favourite candle to represent himself. I offer a choice from the coloured candles, some of which will also have patterns. They may not be tea-light candles but they are always small. We place that candle in the centre of the table, admire it and talk about it for a few minutes. We might talk about why it was the child's favourite, or a time when he remembers a candle. Then I invite the child to choose another special candle to represent someone in his life who is special/important to him. We then decide where we will place it in relation to his candle. Very close by perhaps? We repeat the process of talking about the candle and the person it was chosen for. Repeat this process until all the child's important people have a candle on the table. Stay child-centred if the child names someone as an important person in his life but you don't think that is accurate. Be curious but don't disagree. One teenage boy I was working with told me he chose a special candle 'for this bloke I once met. I dinnae ken his name but he was cool.' I asked why he was special. He stated, 'He telt me ma mither was wrang for battering me and gave me money for a sweet. I was just wee.'

4. Once all the special people have been named, move to use the white candles. Ask the child to light a candle for everybody who knows him. In my experience you will run out of candles before you run out of people, and that is just what you want to happen. Celebrate with the child all the people that he knows and how important he is to these people.

5. Having all the candles burning is a wonderful sight. Encourage the child to enjoy it and emphasise that he has made it happen because he has so many people in his life. Stand back from the table a little and stretch your arms out. Can you feel the soft warm heat? Is that nice? Is that maybe like friendship – comforting and good? Walk as far away from the candles as you can. You can still see them, so even when you are far away, friends and important people are still there. If the child feels safe enough with you, can he close his eyes? Can he picture the candles in his head? Yes? Okay, now can he picture his important person? Yes? So even though that person is not here today they are always with him, right? This can be used in connection with bereavement. Tell the child the next time he feels lonely or is in trouble, maybe he could remember all the candles, then choose one of his important

people to remember and think what that person would do with him if he was there or what would he say about things. This part of this exercise is more suited to older children, but do it with younger children, depending on their development. They can take in a great deal. A child of four announced to her nursery nurse after I had done this exercise with her, 'My mummy's a star now but she is in my head too. I can see her anytime!' (Her mother had died.)

6. Lastly I take a photograph and then we blow out the candles and tidy up. Some children might find this bit hard so it is important to remind them that even when the candles are not lit, they can remember all the people. I might ask the carer of the child to keep a special candle for the child, which they can light together, when needed.

FOLLOW-UP

Get the photograph developed quickly and make a nice frame for it with the child or stick it onto card. Let the child decorate the card and then laminate it.

Chapter 11

Strategies to Use When Carer Breaks Are Required

Prepare for breaks

Children who are looked after away from home deserve a special mention here. It is worth giving careful consideration to how you and the child's carers manage when the carer has a break and the child has to go into respite care. Rather than view this as an unfortunate necessity, I think respite can be a valuable experience for the child, if managed well.

While children bring great pleasure, they can also be hard work. Most parents value a break and usually grandparents, aunts and uncles or close friends will step in, so it should be no surprise that carers need a break, especially if there are additional challenges of attachment or conduct disorders, specialised health needs and so on, which often come with children accommodated away from home. When managed well, respite care can widen the child's social circle, increase her confidence and provide her with more safe people in her life who have different skills and interests.

To have these benefits, respite has to be introduced to the child in a sensitive way; otherwise it can be a source of distress and unsettle a placement. Here are some simple rules:

- Respite should be introduced from the start of the placement. By this I mean that respite carers should be part of the foster family and child's life from day one as friends would be. Ideally the carer should have a photograph of the respite carers in the home and make a point of talking about them. The child should be allowed to get to know the respite carers in the same way as she would get to know relations (with telephone calls, visits, etc.), the aim being to normalise respite and make it part of family life. This is important because the child may read all sorts of things into the temporary move. What did she do to be sent away? Do the foster carers not like her any more? Even with lots of reassurances, if the respite carers have not been introduced at the start of the placement, there is potential for these misconceptions to take root in the child's mind.

- Careful consideration should be given to the timing of the first respite period. Too early, and there is a risk that the foster placement will suffer as the child struggles to adjust to two new homes and tentative attachments are disrupted. Too late, and the child may resent being 'sent away' and struggle to engage positively with the respite carer. Consideration has to be given to the child's needs and current presentation, the respite carer's needs and availability, and the wider picture in terms of what is going on for the child at the time. For example, if there is a lot of stress and change in other areas of the child's life, then introducing a respite period at that point may not be the best timing.

- Preparation for respite care should give time and attention to gradual introductions, as well as ensuring the respite carer knows the child's likes and dislikes, needs at bedtime and so on. The social worker should visit the respite carer independently, and let the child know he has done this, that he approves of the respite carer and knows where the child is going. The social worker should bring back lots of snippets of information to pass to the child in a tone of positive anticipation, 'There's a swing in the garden. Your room there has green curtains.' If appropriate, the parents should also meet the respite carers. If possible, the social worker should visit the child in the respite placement. If not, he should consider leaving a picture or a letter for the child at the respite carers' house.

- Respite care should happen regularly and predictably and be a normal part of life. Then if emergency respite is required it can be managed in a low-key way: 'Jacky and John have asked if they can have you for an extra weekend? How cool is that?'

- Even if the respite is required because of the child's challenging behaviour, this should rarely be conveyed to the child. This behaviour is likely to stem from unmet needs, either historically or currently, so while a child can be helped to be responsible for her behaviour, she is not responsible for its root cause. Managing feelings and behaviour appropriately takes practice. All children get it wrong sometimes, and children who have survived or are surviving difficult life circumstances will get it wrong perhaps more often because of their vulnerabilities, which include coping methods that can be difficult for others to understand or live with. The impact this has on those caring for them can be very significant and often negative. We need to be careful not to punish children for not achieving what are difficult life skills to master.

From a behavioural perspective, if we state openly that carers need respite because of the child's behaviour, we immediately give the power to the child. The problem with this is that it may escalate the problematic behaviour every time the carer challenges the child, for instance, by setting appropriate limits. The child may make a bid to manipulate the situation and gain control by eliciting the predicted response – respite care. This happens because we give the child the message that the people in charge of her cannot contain or hold her. This will almost certainly lead to feelings of being unsafe, as children need to know the adult is firmly in charge. Without this, the child will escalate her behaviour until she finds a boundary in an attempt to find safety.

Activities to reassure on separation

Some children will be openly anxious about separating from a foster carer. Others will appear unaffected and it may be that if they have not made an attachment, they are less affected by the separation. However, the children we work with are often experts at survival, and for them it means hiding emotions from adults and adopting an 'I don't care' attitude. It is better to assume that the child will miss the carers and put in place strategies to ease any potential distress.

- Foster carers could give the respite carer a little gift or note to place under the child's pillow, at the end of the bed or on the door handle, while the child is sleeping. When the child wakes in the morning she can open the surprise.

- Foster carers (and maybe the social worker) could post a letter to the child to arrive during her respite period. This gives the message, 'I am thinking of you and I know where you are' and the child could post something back to the carer – a letter or a picture she has drawn.

- Foster carers could fill a teddy bear up with hugs before the child goes to respite care, and the child could claim these when needed. The child should observe the carer giving the bear multiple hugs and practise claiming them back with the carer.

- If the child is going away for more than two days, the foster carers could make a calendar with windows for the child to open each day she is at the respite carers. Perhaps the social worker could help the child make one for her carers. This gives the message that the foster carers will miss the child too.

- The foster carers could teach the child something special to do. It could be making biscuits with a funny face or a magic trick or how to plant cress. The child could be tasked with the job of teaching this to the respite carers (who have been primed in advance). This is a confidence-building activity. Some children respond well to having a job to do. It also gives permission for the child to talk about her carers in their absence. The respite carer might also like to send the child back home with a new skill. This encourages the idea of the two placements being connected, and carers valuing each other. This should be reinforced with, 'I'm glad John taught you to bake these biscuits, they taste so good.' Used well, this activity can help build self-esteem.

- The child could be given a disposable camera to record her stay, to share when she gets back home. Again, this encourages integration of the two placements and also adds a chapter to the child's life-story book.

- The child could be given a special responsibility while in respite care, such as watering a cactus (as it will not need watering between placements), or turning the calendar over. This could be her special job while there, which no one else does quite so well.

  I worked with a child who declared he *had* to go to respite every month, because if he didn't the male respite carer wouldn't get his 'pizza dinner'. This treat only happened when the child came to stay, and became a responsibility that was taken very seriously. It gave the child permission to go to respite care, and this became very important as the placement went on and the carers (exhausted from caring for the child) really needed a break. The child was reluctant to leave the carers as they 'might miss me too much,' so these wonderful carers were able to remind him that the respite carer needed his 'pizza dinner' and not going would deprive him of this treat.

- The teddy in the cupboard. You could tell the child that the teddy found in the cupboard has only ever lived in this house. He has never been on holiday or gone to live with someone else for a while, and is looking for an adventure. Could the child take him on an adventure? He could go to respite care with the child. Could they pack a bag for him? Have a few teddy accessories ready to pack in a small case. Teddy is excited but also a bit scared. What could they do to reassure teddy that he will be coming back? Does the child think teddy will know he is definitely coming back if he knows he is leaving most of his toys and clothes behind? Could they show teddy the calendar with the date of return marked on it? But most importantly, teddy knows he can trust the child to bring him back.

- The main carer could record her voice or make a video reading a favourite story.

- The child could borrow a small amount of the main carer's favourite scent to take with her. Smell is very important in attachment, and a small amount on a pillowcase or soft toy or even the child's clothes can bring reassurance.

- The child could take her comfort box and if appropriate, her safety shield (see pp.164–66 and pp.153–56 respectively).

Chapter 12

Strategies to Help with Night-time Difficulties

Fears around going to bed or having disturbed sleep are common issues among the children and young people I work with. Children need good routines. Predictable and safe behaviour from adults (to match the child's developmental stage) is required by all children, but especially children with fears at bedtime.

Focus on how you, as a social worker or helping adult, can support a child with bedtime fears.

The following are a series of resources and activities I have used. Many are very simple and straightforward but effective. This is not an exhaustive list of ideas to help around bedtime, but just a few that I use on a regular basis.

Picture books

Hutchins, P. (1972, 2012) *Good-night Owl!* London: Simon & Schuster. This is a story of an owl that can't sleep at night due to noise.

Murphy, J. (1980) *Peace at Last.* London: Picturemacs. A story about a bear trying to get to sleep and being tired in the morning because of lack of sleep.

Brown, R. (1981) *Dark, Dark Tale.* London: Hippo Books. An exciting, possibly scary tale about a cat exploring an old house in the dark.

Kerr, J. (1993) *Mog on Fox Night.* London: Collins. A story about Mog the cat who doesn't want his tea and is put outside overnight. He encounters foxes. This is a gentle story.

East, H. and Sanders, J. (1987) *Down in the Dark.* London: MacDonald & Company. A story about a little girl who hears a noise in the night and is scared. She goes to investigate and discovers it is a dog.

Hessell, J. (1989) *Staying at Sam's.* London: Picture Lions. A story about a child who goes for an overnight stay at a friend's house and discovers that bedtime routines are different.

Waddell, M. and Benson, P. (1992) *Owl Babies.* London: Walker Books. A story about owl babies wakening to find that their mother has left the nest to go hunting. They are all worried but try hard to reassure each other.

All of the above are aimed at younger children. Remember to assess the child's developmental stage, not age. If you are not sure, ask the child to help you to do a book review so that you can decide which one to use with younger children. You will soon build up your own library of favourite stories by asking parents what their children enjoy and having a search in the children's section of the local library (librarians can be very helpful in identifying popular books) and second-hand shops.

Or you could suggest that it would be good to write a book together and maybe a way to begin would be to read some stories to see if you can get some ideas. These suggestions allow the child to decide whether the story is age-appropriate or not, by their response to it. If it is too young for them, you have avoided insulting or embarrassing them.

Books for older children are hard to find. They tend to have more text and fewer pictures, which is unhelpful for children who find reading hard work. They also don't feed the imagination in the same way, being composed of more words than pictures.

The important thing to remember is that regardless of the child's stage of development, books are just a basic resource to allow you to introduce a subject. By extending this resource into play you will create opportunities for the child to talk about personal experiences and to problem solve.

Try making the child's favourite character from a story. Young children will be happy to make a simple model using any materials to hand. It may not look much like the chosen character to an adult, but this doesn't matter. The activity of making and talking is the important thing. Older children tend to want their models to bear some resemblance to the image in the book, however, so provide a few items that are specific to that character. For example, you could draw some cartoon eyes for them to stick on, or provide feathers if they are making a baby owl.

Some other ideas

- Paint a picture of a character from the book or make a puppet.

- Make a scene from the book. I use the cardboard trays that tins and cans are displayed on in supermarkets. The best scenes tend to emerge when children build them on these trays out of any bits and pieces. If you can work in a playroom or kitchen area, papier-mâché is fantastic and is very tactile. Plasticine, clay and homemade playdough also work well.

- Once the scene is finished the children can play out the story, and perhaps at a later date, build a model of their own room and play out what happens at bedtime or during the night. Many children I have worked with do this quite spontaneously, often using the model they have built but just adapting it slightly. You can suggest that they may wish to do this, but never push – remain child-centred. It is important that they have had the experience of playing out a fictitious story first as it gives them the chance to experiment before exploring a personal and potentially very emotive experience.

- Make up your own story. As suggested earlier, support the child to write his own story. He could perhaps write one for younger children, or write a leaflet for parents, carers and social workers about how to help children with fears at nightime. Perhaps he might like to draw a cartoon strip.

- Make up a short play. Try enlisting the help of a few favourite cuddly toys or brothers, sisters and parents (if willing), and place the child in the position of director. This can easily be developed into solution-focused work. For example, view the child's work as Scene one and invite suggestions from other cast members for Scene two, which might have a different outcome from Scene one. One of the parents I worked with directed Scene two and wove into the story the mother-figure buying a night light with the child. The child spontaneously acted out an enthusiastic response. The outcome of this was the next day the parents bought a night light and put it in the child's room. The child reported that the monsters couldn't get her as they only liked the dark. As the family's worker I had been suggesting a night light for at least a fortnight, but had met fierce resistance from the parents. Perhaps the night light was much more effective because in the child's eyes, it was mum and dad who thought of and bought it.

- Use free play to help with sleep problems. Ensure that you provide some items in your free play choices that lend themselves to discussion about sleep. So, in a playroom, I always have a house area with a bed and a blanket. I often need to travel with my toys, so I have a little wooden box with a mouse puppet tucked into it. I always have a small torch (the kind you attach to a key ring) in my bag, and in my car I have a travel rug. I also have a bag of doll's house figures and furniture that includes, you guessed it, a bed! I also have some of the books listed above. Now if bedtime is on a child's mind he has the possibility of using these toys to play out his experiences and to prompt conversation. You can apply the same logic to other issues, for instance, a new baby in the home, and provide appropriate play materials for that situation.

- If the child has a favourite teddy it is obviously important he gets to take it to bed. You could put some of mum's perfume on teddy or dress it in a t-shirt of dad's. This is based on an understanding that attachment is built on sensory experience. The smell of a familiar and trusted person will bring comfort. Do check that the child's special teddy has not been removed from him as a punishment, or that the parent is not threatening this. In itself this can be enough to completely disrupt a child's bedtime and sleep routine, and I have come across this punishment several times. It is okay to remove a favourite toy as a sanction, but this should not be the toy that is the child's comforter at bedtime.

• Tuck the children up tightly! Babies settle more easily when swaddled. The feeling of containment – being held – gives a sense of security and safety.

• Install a baby monitor. It can be helpful for the child to have some verbal communication to provide reassurance without the need to get out of bed, especially if included in a behaviour management strategy. I have also used a baby monitor with older children who have night-time separation anxieties. In this case the monitors were placed in the young person's bedroom and the sitting room, on a low volume, which allowed the young person to hear the background noise of the TV and the carer/parents chatting, providing reassurance that they were not alone.

• Make an audio-recording of the carer reading a story and place it on repeat. Very soon the child will not be listening to the story, just the rhythm of the attachment figure's voice, which is comforting. Most children grow out of the need for this reassurance once they feel safe and settled.

• Leave a bit of you behind. When you are accommodating a child away from home on an emergency basis, try and make sure he has his important things with him. However, I have removed children late at night in volatile circumstances when the best practice you can manage is to get them out safely. In situations like this ensure that you leave a part of you with the child – a transitional object. This would be the most effective if the child had an established relationship with you, but do it anyway, even if the child doesn't know you. It can do no harm and if the child views you as his rescuer, it could even do some good. An advantage to always travelling with toys is that I have plenty of transitional objects, but the scarf you are wearing or a necklace, etc. will work equally well. Ask the child to look after it for you until you come back. This will help him not to feel abandoned.

- Remind the carer that the child may never have had a bedtime routine, and help the carer make up a cartoon strip of a bedtime routine in this house for the child to refer to and, of course, if you know anything of the child's bedtimes at home, tell the carer.

- A word of caution: be careful when using torches. They can produce shadows and also only light up one area of the room, leaving dark corners, so it may be better to use a soft night light.

Practice example

One little boy, aged seven, told me there were monsters living under his bed. When I asked what they looked like, I was told they were green, hairy and one had a big toenail.

Me: 'Oh dear, that sounds like a serious problem. How many are there?'

Child: 'Usually two or three.'

Me: 'Are they always there?' (This is the exception question. I want to know if I can find a time when the problem doesn't exist and why that is.)

Child: 'Yes.'

Me: 'Are there any times they are not scary?'

Child: 'Yes.'

Me: 'That's interesting. What's different about those nights?'

Child: 'Gran's here. Dad's with his friends.'

Me: 'Okay. So why do you think they are not scary when gran is here?'

Child: "Cos gran reads a story at bedtime like mum used to.'

Me: 'So mum used to read a story when you were in bed and gran still does this, but dad doesn't and the monsters get upset and are scary when there is no bedtime story.'

Child: 'Yeah, that's it. Dad tells them go away then they go away but when he goes to sleep they come back and I waken him and then he says just go to sleep will you, there is no such thing as monsters, stop being a baby.'

I am sure you have spotted the problem. Usually monsters, ghosts and things that go bump in the night, all serve a purpose in life. I could have just simply asked the father to read a bedtime story, but I am almost certain this would not have worked. This child's mother had died and the father was coping with his own grief by keeping busy and 'getting the kids to grow up a bit'. This child needed to adjust to the idea of losing his monsters and losing the excuse to waken his father each night. This brought the child much needed individual attention (there were four siblings), even though it was negative attention. So I needed to change this behaviour slowly.

Me: 'Okay, we clearly have two green hairy monsters, one with a big toenail, who need to be dealt with. I think it will take at least five nights and will need my magic water spray (child listening intently) and it will only work if you really want them to go and if you do exactly what I say. What do you think?'

Child: 'I don't want them under my bed no more.'

Me: 'I will go back to my office and bring my magic water. You will need to spray it under your bed every night before you get into bed and at the same time shout, "Go away hairy green monsters. I don't need you." Could you do that? It's quite hard.'

Child: 'I could do that. It's no hard.'

I left the family and went to buy a plastic spray bottle to hold the 'magic' water. I then drew a label with a green hairy monster, a red monster and blue monster on it, put a black line through them and stuck it to the bottle. Underneath I wrote, 'Makes all kinds of monsters leave.' I didn't put any message that suggested the monster would be harmed as some children may quite like their imaginary friend.

Returning to the family home I presented this bottle to the child in front of his siblings and his father, who took charge of the bottle until bedtime. I then spoke to the father alone and asked him to reinstate the bedtime story. He didn't want to, so I made an agreement with him that if the monsters didn't leave in ten days, and the child was still waking him, he could stop. I explained to the little boy that his father had agreed to do this, but that he was a beginner at reading bedtime stories, so if he enjoyed the story he should be sure to tell his father, so that he knew he was getting it right.

It took eight days for the monsters to vacate that house, so there was a bit of resistance, but in the end, they did go. The bedtime story was a great success, with the father enjoying it too. It also helped him agree to go to an adult literacy skills course.

Instructions for Making Your Own Playdough and Glup

Playdough
What you need

- 3 tablespoons of cooking oil.
- 2 cups of flour.
- 1 cup of salt.
- 2 cups of water.
- Food colouring (optional).
- Food essence or essential oil (optional).
- Saucepan.

What to do

1. Place the cooking oil, water, food colouring and food essence (if you are using them) in a saucepan. Add the flour and salt.
2. Place the pan on a low heat and keep stirring. Do not leave it unattended.
3. The mixture will begin to form into a ball. When there is no liquid left, remove from the heat and tip out onto a work surface. Be careful as it will be hot.
4. Leave it to cool until you can comfortably knead the dough well. When it is cold it is ready to use.

Keep the playdough stored in a sealed tub in the fridge.

✓

Glup (Gloop or Slime)

What you need

- 1 packet of cornflour (enough for two to three people to play with).

- Water.

- Food colouring (optional; if using, be careful how it is used as it stains).

- Big basin.

What to do

1. Place the cornflour in the big basin and gradually add water, mixing with your hands as you go. Once all the cornflour is wet, you have glup.

After playing with glup (it is messy, but fun), clean surfaces with hot water. If the glup goes on the carpet or on clothes, leave until it is dry and it will brush off.

Ideas for Memory Questions Activity and 'Getting to Know You' Games

I wish...	People like me because...	It's scary when...
Why do I...?	I hate...	Tomorrow I want to...
I feel angry when...	The most important person in my life just now is...	I am good at...
Things feel okay when I am...	I feel happy when...	I want you to...
If I had money I would...	I feel ill when...	If I could change one thing in my life, it would be...
You can help me by...	In two years' time I hope...	School is...
I feel violent when...	If I had the power to grant someone a wish I would give that wish to...	I would like it if there was a machine that could...
Being at home is...	My dream pet would be...	The person who most often upsets me is...

Whose Job? Cards

Open the mail	Make tea
Wash clothes	Keep things safe
Collect medicine	Wash dishes
Buy food	Give out bus fares
Make breakfast	Get to school
Help with worries	Help with homework
Provide treats	Buy presents
Look after the pets	Keep the noise down
Make the beds	Decide what to watch on TV
Keep me safe	Speak to social worker
Make a doctor's appointment	Keep the fridge clean
Buy clothes	Boil the kettle
Use the microwave	Bake a birthday cake
Order a takeaway	Lock the door at night
Watch the baby	Help me get to clubs and groups
Decide who visits	Give cuddles
Tell me when to have a shower/bath	Make sure I have soap and toothpaste
Help me when I hurt myself	

The Tree

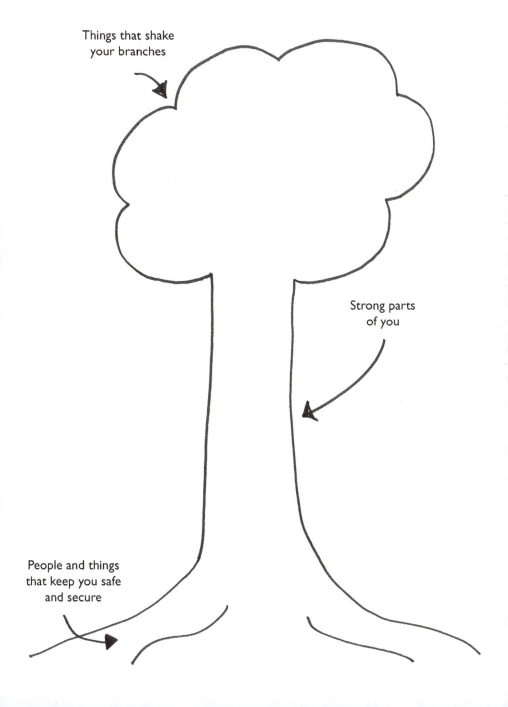

Things that shake
your branches

Strong parts
of you

People and things
that keep you safe
and secure

✓

Appendix V
Spider's Web

If the bird ate the spider and all the problems
disappeared, what would life be like/feel like?

Spider's Web 2

The problem is that the spider is inside the web and the bird can't get at it. What is stopping you get at the spider – change your situation?

Spider's Web 3

Who, or what, can help get at the spider? What will clear the web away?

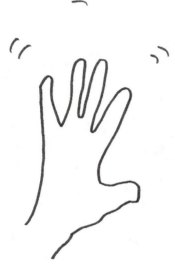

Emotional Literacy Cards

My balloon escaped!	I've got an ice-cream
I was told off! No!	My teddy is broken
I was given a present	My dog died

Cartooning

Thinking box	
Action box. [You can add speech bubbles if you wish]	
♡ Feeling box	♡
♡	♡
♡	♡

Faces Depicting Emotions

Glossary

Active listening: placing full attention on the client and showing interest by body posture and affirming vocalisations.

Directed play: often called structured play. Guiding play with specific learning intentions in mind. Many of the activities in this book use directed play.

Occupational play: play which is purely to occupy the child, for instance assorted toys provided in a waiting room or the colouring sheets for children often given out by airlines or restaurants.

Free play: where the child plays freely with whatever they wish and in any way they want. The adult may support by providing materials and ensuring safety but does not interfere in any other way with the child's play.

Small world imaginative play: the use of toys which help recreate life experiences on a small scale e.g. a doll's house; a zoo or farm set; a fire station etc. and toy figures. The child uses their knowledge of the world and/or their imagination to repeat familiar scenario and test out ideas in a bid to make sense of these. This supports their learning and development.

Scaling tool: an item or 'tool' which can be used to help people scale their response to a question or situation in order of impact. (See p.111 for how to make one).

Person centred counselling: an approach which believes the solution to a problem lies with the client/patient/individual and the role of the counsellor is to support the individual to facilitate change. See the work of Carl Rogers.

Task centred practice: identifying and working on specific problems identified by the worker/counsellor and client.

Self-sabotaging: behaviour which either consciously or unconsciously limits change.

Soft play: play areas which offer climbing and play equipment that is soft i.e. made of foam or plastic.

Transitional object: a thing (toy or personal item) used by a child for consolation in the absence of the owner.

Solution focused therapy: a strengths-based approach which uses the inner resources people possess in order to assist the change process. It concentrates on brief intervention and uses tools such as scaling and the exception and miracle questions (Turnell & Edwards 1999).

Bibliography

Ainsworth, M.D.S., Blehar, M., Aters, E. and Wall, S. (1978) *Patterns of Attachment: A Psychological Study of the Strange Situation*. Hillsdale, NJ: Lawrence Erlbaum.

Anning, A. and Ring, K. (2004) *Making Sense of Children's Drawings*. Maidenhead: Open University Press.

Benson, J. (2009) *Working More Creatively with Groups*. London: Routledge.

Case, C. and Dalley, T. (eds) (1990) *Working with Children in Art Therapy*. London and New York: Tavistock/Routledge.

Daniel, B., Wassell, S. and Gilligan, R. (1999) *Child Development for Child Care and Protection Workers*. London: Jessica Kingsley Publishers.

De Jong, P. and Berg, I.K. (2008) *Interviewing for Solutions*. 3rd edition. Pacific Grove, CA: Thomson Brooks/Cole.

Egan, G. (2001) *The Skilled Helper*. Pacific Grove, CA: Brooks/Cole.

Fahlberg, V.I. (1991) *A Child's Journey through Placement*. Indianapolis, IN: Perspectives Press.

Freeman, J., Epston, D. and Lobovits, D. (1997) *Playful Approaches to Serious Problems: Narrative Therapy with Children and their Families*. New York: W.W. Norton.

Gerhardt, S. (2004) *Why Love Matters*. London: Routledge.

Gross, R. (2010) *Psychology: The Science of Mind and Behaviour*. London: Hodder Education.

Jarrett, C. (1982) *Helping Children Cope with Separation and Loss*. Boston, MA: Harvard Common Press.

Kerr, J. (1993) *Mog on Fox Night*. London: Collins.

Lishman, J. (1991) *Handbook of Theory for Practice Teachers in Social Work*. London: Jessica Kingsley Publishers.

McMahon, L. (2009) *The Handbook of Play Therapy and Therapeutic Play*. 2nd edition. London and New York: Routledge.

Ratey, J. (2001) *A User's Guide To The Brain*. London: Little, Brown & Company.

Redgrave, K. (2000) *Care-therapy for Children: Direct Work in Counselling and Psychotherapy*. London: Continuum.

Rogers, C.R. (2003) *Client Centred Therapy: Its Current Practice, Implications and Theory*. London: Constable.

Ross, D. (2001) *I Fought at Bannockburn*. London: Corgi.

Salans, M. (2004) *Storytelling with Children in Crisis*. London: Jessica Kingsley Publishers.

Schore, A. (1994) *Affect Regulation and the Origin of the Self*, Hillsdale, NJ: Lawrence Erlbaum.

Turnell, A. and Edwards, S. (1999) *Signs of Safety: A Solution and Safety Oriented Approach to Child Protection Casework*. New York: W.W. Norton.

Index